Contents

RUGBY TRAINING

Peter Winder

A & C Black · London

First published 1990 by
A & C Black (Publishers) Ltd
35 Bedford Row, London WC1R 4JH

ISBN 0 7136 3267 4

A CIP catalogue record for this book is
available from the British Library.

Acknowledgements
Photographs: Associated Sports
Photography (pp. 59, 77, 83, 90/1, 93, 100,
103); Action-Plus Photographic (pp. 50, 63);
Supersport Photographs (p. 4); Sporting
Pictures (UK) Ltd (cover).
All line drawings by Neil Sutton.

Printed and bound in Great Britain by
Courier International, Tiptree, Essex

Introduction

Rugby football has a universal appeal to sports enthusiasts because the organisation of the game provides the opportunity for players of all shapes and sizes to make an important contribution. There are 15 specialist positions in a rugby team and each one requires a player with a different range of physical attributes, individual talents and skills.

There are general aspects of the game that all participants need to master; rugby football is a physical contact sport and players must be prepared physically and mentally to meet the demands of a game situation.

Nurturing the desire of each player to acquire the fitness and master the relevant techniques to enable him to participate successfully in a game should be the objective of every good rugby coach. Instilling sound technical development during coaching sessions will form the basic foundation and launching point for producing players of ability and must be the priority of all coaches.

Initially the coach needs to concentrate on organising practices that will provide the players with the opportunity of acquiring and mastering the basic skills. Every session should be enjoyable, rewarding and structured to provide continuity and development for the participants. Working with the ball motivates players to extend themselves, but coaches should plan each session to include valuable stretching and fitness work as well.

A good rugby coach will be organised and plan practice sessions to extend the players' knowledge, experience and abilities. This publication highlights the key features of rugby football and provides a selection of fundamental skill practices and ideas for coaching sessions.

Note Throughout the book players and coaches are referred to individually as 'he'. This should of course be taken to mean 'he or she' where appropriate.

Left *Great Britain versus France*

Basic principles of playing and coaching

Principles of play

Rugby football is a team game that involves 15 players contributing as two distinct units, eight forwards and seven three-quarters. The objective of the game is for the players to secure and retain possession of the ball, and capitalise by scoring enough points to win the game.

Scoring points, whether by means of a try or a successful kick at goal, is not a simple matter of placing the ball over the goal line or kicking it through the posts, but requires conformity to the laws of the game. Creating scoring opportunities during a game requires the players to perform with a common purpose and direction within the constraints of the laws. Selecting and employing the correct tactics and strategies that exploit time and space to gain a numerical advantage over the players' opponents forms the basis of an effective performance.

The forwards are generally considered to be the ball-winning unit of the team, consisting of combative players whose strength, fitness, durability, applied techniques and skills secure possession of the ball for their team at line-outs, scrummages, rucks and mauls. Whether the forwards win or lose possession of the ball, they are required to drive their opponents backwards, helping to create space and opportunities for their team-mates to exploit, or attempting to disrupt the quality of the possession secured by their opponents.

The three-quarters are the unit of players entrusted to use the hard-earned possession effectively, with their quick, elusive and penetrative running, passing and kicking skills. The backs are required to utilise the possession, help to create good attacking positions for the team to exploit, and prevent their opponents from scoring any points or crossing the advantage line.

The role of the coach

To play rugby football, each player needs to be physically fit, mentally alert, familiar with the rules of the game and able to execute the fundamental skills: running with and passing the ball, tackling opponents in possession and competing for the possession of the ball. The coach's role is to prepare players for the demands of competition.

Players are very dependent on one another during the game, and the coach's task is to prepare and harness the talents of the individual players into a successful team effort. The coach must organise, co-ordinate and harmonise the forwards and three-quarters into an effective team of two individual but cohesive units. The coach must be a dominant character during training and practice sessions.

Team selection, formations and patterns of play require careful consideration by the coach; the tactics employed by the team should complement the abilities and skills of the available players. Within the team formation there will always be an opportunity for individual expression and creativity during a game situation. A good coach will encourage players to attempt to exploit any opportunity that arises during the transitional periods of a competitive game.

The most important quality that a coach must possess is the ability to successfully communicate ideas, thoughts and instructions to the players. Establishing and developing a good rapport with players requires considerable personality, and a coach needs to possess many diverse qualities, including adaptability, sincerity, patience, persistence, humour, consistency, diplomacy, sensitivity, discipline and integrity, all encompassed in a dynamic and enthusiastic approach.

The position of coach is a highly rewarding, enjoyable and influential one, demanding responsibility, commitment, dedication, forward planning and sound organisation. The major responsibility of a coach is the planning and organisation of regular, purposeful and challenging practice sessions. The ability to analyse faults and initiate practices to rectify them will improve the players' performances and consequently encourage them to extend the range of techniques and skills necessary for their successful participation in rugby football.

Physical conditioning and fitness work

To meet the demands of rugby football – a hard, physical, collision sport – players must be conditioned and prepared for its fitness requirements. When preparing and planning sessions, a coach should always allocate time for stretching and warm-up activities and should stress the importance of these exercises to the players.

All players are frustrated when injury prevents them from participating in competitive games, but they never seem to devote the same meticulous approach to training that they allocate to their preparations before a game. Many players have individual superstitions and routines to which they rigidly adhere on match days, to prepare them mentally and physically for the challenges of the game. However, they approach training with a far more cavalier attitude, commencing strenuous physical exercise and contact practices without warming up correctly.

Coaches must insist that players warm up properly before commencing any training or participating in any practice sessions. Stressing the importance of stretching and encouraging players to establish a routine of warm-up exercises will benefit everyone, preparing them for the exertions to follow. It will probably reduce the number of injuries that occur to players.

Warming up and stretching

All players can improve their performance by increasing the range, flexibility and mobility of muscles and joints. Participating in a sequence of stretching and warm-up exercises will also begin to focus the players' attention on the key features of the practices or to prepare for the forthcoming game. Each series of stretches and warm-up activities should be demanding and challenging, but varied and stimulating.

Once players are educated about the value of a good warm-up and period of stretching exercises, the coach can progress to specific fitness programmes that are relevant to the particular needs of the players. It is necessary to warm up the important joints of the body and to stretch all of the main muscle groups in preparation for each training session. The sequence of exercises below will help to prepare players for their participation in rugby practices.

Upper body

Trunk stretch

Stand with your feet shoulder width apart; stretch each arm and hand in turn as far as possible down the same side of the body, aiming to reach beyond the knee. It is important that the back remains straight, with the shoulders pushed backwards. The head moves sideways only, to help to extend the reach fully. Do not move the head forwards, otherwise the spine will not remain straight.

Develop this exercise by:
1 walking the fingers of both hands as far down the back of the thighs as possible by arching the spine and tilting the head backwards
2 walking the hands down the front of each thigh on to the feet and along the ground until the body is in a prone position, supported by the hands as well as the feet. Continue to 'walk' the fingers along the ground, reaching as far as possible beyond the head before returning to the start position via the same method in reverse.

Trunk rotation

Again stand with your feet shoulder width apart, keeping the spine and head upright and the shoulders pushed back. Hold both elbows level with the shoulders and bend the forearms high across the chest. Turn the head and body to complete a full quarter turn of the trunk. Straighten the leading arm and push it as far behind the body as possible. Further rotation of the body will be achieved when the head is also turned to watch the fingers, extending the range of shoulder joint movement. Return to the start position and repeat in the opposite direction.

Head rotation

Stand with your feet shoulder width apart, keeping the spine and head upright. Turn the head slowly from side to side as far as possible, attempting to turn the head further on each attempt. Do not rotate the head in a circular movement, and keep the chin held away from the chest.

Pectoral muscles

Stand with your legs shoulder width apart, keeping the spine and head upright and the shoulders pushed back. Hold both elbows level with the shoulders and the forearms high across the chest. Push the elbows backwards twice before flinging both arms out and backwards as far as possible. Keep the elbows and arms level with the shoulders and parallel to the ground.

Arm rotation

Stand with the feet shoulder width apart and the arms outstretched to the side of the body, level with the shoulders and parallel to the ground. Turn the palms downwards. With the fingers and arms extended and straight, rotate the wrists backwards and forwards so that the palms face alternately up and then down.

Develop this exercise by keeping the wrists still and the arms very straight. Rotate the arms backwards to draw small circles with the tips of the fingers. Gradually and very slowly increase the range of the movement to draw progressively larger circles, pausing at different stages to concentrate on the size of the circle. Continue the exercise until the shoulders are rotating through their full range of movement, with the fingers touching the ears and then the thighs as they complete the circles. After a short rest, repeat this exercise, rotating the arms forwards to draw the different-sized circles. Always keep the arms straight, level with the shoulders and parallel to the ground, with the wrists locked.

Hamstrings

Leg stretch
Squat down, placing the fingers of each hand under the toes of the foot on that side of the body. Slowly straighten the legs, keeping the fingers under the toes. Hold the stretch position for a period; initially this should be short but it can be varied and extended.

Touch your toes
Stand with your feet shoulder width apart, reach down and across with the left hand to touch the right foot. Return to the start position, then repeat by touching the left foot with the right hand. It is important that the legs remain straight; if this limits the ability to touch the feet, then reach down as far as possible. This exercise can also be undertaken while sitting on the ground.

Outward walk
Stand with your legs shoulder width apart, keeping the spine and head upright and the shoulders pushed back. Start to slowly walk the feet outwards as far as possible. Hold the stance before walking the feet back to the start position. Keep the upper body straight at all times; do not lean forwards or lose balance by walking the feet too wide apart.

Split stretch
Place one leg in front of the other and stand with the legs as far apart as possible, keeping both feet flat on the ground. With the hands on the hips, bend the front knee to support the body weight, while keeping the back leg straight. Hold this stretch position before turning to the other side to repeat the exercise, stretching the other hamstring and calf muscles.

Sitting hurdle
Sit on the ground in the hurdle position, with the left leg outstretched and the right leg bent at right angles to the body. Hold the left ankle with both hands

and pull the upper body down towards the foot, attempting to touch the knee with the nose. Hold the position when the head is as close to the leg as possible. Return to the starting position, change the leg positions and repeat the exercise to extend the muscles on the other side of the body.

Stomach and lower back

Sit-up
Lie on your back with the arms behind the head, the legs bent at the knees and the feet flat on the ground. Raise the upper body to a sitting position, touching the knees with the elbows before returning to the start position. Always keep the knees bent during this exercise.

Develop this exercise by including a rotation of the upper body when raised in the sitting position. Alternate the sides which the body is turned towards on each sit-up until it is possible to rotate to both sides before returning to the start position.

Further extend this exercise by working with a partner. Lie on the ground with your arms stretched out along the ground behind your head. Raise both legs for the partner to hold and support on his thigh. Pull yourself up to touch your feet before returning to the start position. Complete an agreed number of repetitions before changing places with your partner.

Back arches
Lie on your front with your hands behind the head. Raise the head, shoulders and upper body as high as possible keeping the legs and feet on the ground. Hold this position before lowering to the start position and repeating the exercise.

Upright cycling
Lie on your back with the hips and legs in the air, supported by the hands and the arms. Rotate the legs in a cycling movement several times in one direction before repeating the movement in the other direction.

Leg change (back)
Lie on your back with both legs raised off the ground, the left leg stretched out straight and the right leg bent towards the chest. Keep the toes pointed away from the body and change the leg positions quickly. This exercise is similar to the inverted bicycling action, but it stretches a different muscle group.

Legs

Leg raise
Lie on your back with arms alongside the body. Keep both legs straight and

raise the left foot off the ground, pointing the toes away from the body. Slowly return the leg towards the ground but do not return to the start position. Complete this movement 20 times before changing to exercise the right leg.

Develop this exercise by moving the raised leg out to the side before lowering.

This exercise can be further developed by working with a partner to create a gentle resistance to push and pull against when the leg is being raised, moved to the side and lowered to the ground. Both legs must be kept straight during these exercises. The idea of the resistance is to make the player work harder, not to prevent the movement from being completed correctly.

Side leg raise

Lie on your side with one arm stretched out under the head and the other helping to balance the body. Keeping the legs straight and the toes pointed, raise the top leg as high as possible. Hold the position, then repeat the exercise 20 times before changing position to work the other leg.

Develop this exercise by raising the top leg, holding the high position and raising the other leg up to touch the top one, before lowering both of them to the ground again. Repeat this exercise 20 times before changing position to work the other leg.

Heel raise

Stand upright and balance on your left leg. Raise the heel as high as possible off the ground; pause and lower the heel. Repeat this exercise 20 times before changing position to work the calf muscles of the right leg.

Leg change (front)

Support the body on the arms and put the feet in the prone position, starting with one leg straight and the other bent. Keeping the back straight, alter the position of the legs as quickly as possible.

Fitness is specific

Excellent physical conditioning and fitness are vital components of the preparation of all rugby players who hope to maintain a valuable contribution for the duration of a game. Because the performance requirements of each unit and each individual player differ, it is important to identify the roles and contribution that is expected of each player during a game and to prepare physical conditioning and fitness sessions accordingly. Muscular endurance and stamina are the foundation of fitness work for all players.

It is important that all fitness practices contain as many realistic features, including running and handling activities, as possible. Once the demands of the tasks have been mastered the coach must set realistic targets, such as time limits, for the completion of the practices. By means of demanding practice sessions that improve familiarity with the ball in competitive situations, the players can develop fitness that is specific to the requirements of their position.

To prevent any discord among the players or between the units, the coach must make sure that the sessions start and finish with all of the players working together, co-operating and contributing to the team effort. The different units must be given an opportunity to demonstrate their particular strengths, abilities and expertise to one another. Highlighting the specific elements that are involved in each position will help to establish a respectful relationship between the players. Involving all players from time to time in practices that are specific to each unit will prove a valuable experience, helping players to acquire an understanding of and familiarity with the demands of each playing position.

As well as passing and running, the forwards compete for the possession of the ball in the set piece plays of scrummages and line-outs, and in the transitional phases of rucks and mauls. Therefore the fitness work of the forwards has to be extensive; it should be modified and specialised to improve the support play, physical strength and explosive power needed to fulfil the forwards' diverse roles.

Coaches should not allow players to rest for more than 40 seconds before commencing the next activity, because statistical analysis has shown that this is the maximum rest period during a game.

Fitness practices

Every coaching session should commence with a team warm up, consisting of a selection of smooth stretching exercises that will prepare muscles and joints, increasing their suppleness and mobility. This in turn will generally contribute to an improved level of fitness and will positively influence playing performance. Once players are suitably prepared for more vigorous exercises and fitness work, they can participate in demanding group and unit practices. The challenge of working with other players can help to focus attention on the demands of the set tasks.

Activities must always be competitive, with the players working against the clock or with a partner whom each recognises as being relatively similar in ability. Players are motivated to train in a more determined manner when their performance is being recorded or when they are training with a partner whom they acknowledge as a worthwhile opponent. When one player has a distinct advantage over his partner, neither applies himself assiduously to the practice. The set tasks can prove inadequate for the needs of both participants because they are not demanding enough for the stronger player and the lack of success demoralises the weaker one. Therefore any mismatches of players should be carefully avoided at all times by the coach.

Fitness is a very important aspect for the coach to consider, because during the playing of a game, both forwards and backs are involved in running several kilometres/miles at different speeds, either in possession or pursuit of the ball.

Therefore every coaching session should contain many passing and running activities that are relevant to the many different game situations. It is impossible to establish and maintain a running rhythm during a game because the players have to sprint, jog and walk over varying distances in a number of different situations. Therefore all fitness preparation must be relevant to these requirements.

There is no substitute for game-related practices that involve running and the execution of a range of different techniques and skills. They establish the stamina and fitness required to enable players to participate and be influential throughout the whole of a game. Physical conditioning can improve the standards of performance because players will be able to concentrate more easily on the essential aspects of their particular contribution to the game.

Fitness work can be supplemented by carefully structured and controlled weight-training programmes, which can contribute to the development of muscular endurance. This improves strength and power, and also benefits speed training.

Coaches should consider a fitness programme as a schedule of three parts, with each applying to different periods of the year: the close season, when players are not playing rugby: pre-season; and during the months of competitive games.

Training during the close season

Because of the very physical nature of rugby football, the close season provides players with a much-needed opportunity for rest and recuperation after the exertions of a long playing season. All players will obviously benefit from a period of inactivity, but it is unwise to extend this period until the start of pre-season training. During the close season the coach can structure individual training programmes for players that will help to maintain a basis of general fitness, mobility and strength. The programmes may include exercises for all of the muscle groups and specific ones relevant to each playing position.

It is always necessary to establish a routine of suitable warm-up and stretching exercises, preparing the body and mind for the physical and mental exertions of the intended training programme.

After a period of sufficient inactivity, all players need to commence an organised training schedule towards the end of May or the beginning of June. The close-season training programme should contain exercises and practices that can improve the playing abilities of each player. It is an important role of the coach to identify any physical or technical aspects of individual players that need to be improved. The reasons for the problem can be discussed with the player, hopefully resulting in an intensive and concentrated training schedule, planned by both the coach and player to help to eradicate any weakness that might limit performance.

For example, towards the end of the playing season a front-row forward may start to experience scrummaging difficulties. Discussion would establish the reasons for the lack of success and help to agree a suitable training programme that would include relevant exercises to improve the player's stamina and scrummaging power. In this case, an individual training schedule including weight-training exercises would build and strengthen the necessary muscle groups.

Sample programme for a prop forward

After a short break of a few weeks from the exertions of the competitive season, resume training with a warm-up and distance run of 6.5 to 10 km (four to six miles). At the end of the run complete the following exercise schedule to tone the muscles, ligaments and joints, gently re-introducing the body to the demands of training:

Pyramids of overarm/underarm pull-ups: 5:4:3:2:1, then 1:2:3:4:5

  20 sit-ups
  20 back arches
  20 press-ups
  20 squat thrusts
  20 step ups

Continue this programme for a couple of weeks, training every third day and gradually increasing the distance of the run to 13 km (eight miles). At the same time reduce the rest period between the exercises.

When the schedule can be completed without a significant rest pause between the change-over period for each exercise, begin a daily Fartlek training programme on a rota basis:

  1–5 km (1 mile) at a jog
  5 km (3 miles) at a fast pace
  10 × 100 m (yard) sprints
  complete exercise schedule
  1.5 km (1 mile) at a jog

Vary the content of the running, changing and mixing up the order of the activities to include runs at half pace, three-quarter pace, even walking at times to recover but do not reduce the distance; occasionally run five miles against the clock, recording the time for future comparison. Gradually increase the number of repetitions of the exercise schedule until the player can complete three repetitions of the series of exercises.

From then on, every third day the five miles of Fartlek running and exercising can be substituted with an indoor weight-training programme. Again it is vitally important to warm up the muscles, ligaments and joints correctly before commencing any exercises involving weights.

The reason for including weights in the training programme is to improve endurance, power and muscular strength. Particular emphasis must be given to the larger muscle groups used during a combative performance, that is, the legs, back, shoulders, chest, neck and arms. Each exercise must be completed in a series of ten repetitions before going on to the next.

The high pull-up

A wide grip is necessary to raise the bar up to the chin. Move the hips slightly forwards as the bar is raised and take the heels off the ground to support the body weight on the toes. Continue the exercise in a smooth and continuous rhythm, initially with low weights on the bar.

The high pull-up

The power clean and press

Power clean and press

Lift the weight by straightening the legs and extending the back at speed, pulling with the arms once the bar reaches the thighs. Pause with the bar resting on the chest, bend the legs and in one movement raise the bar above the head by straightening the arms and the legs. Hold the weights in this position for a few seconds before returning to the start position.

Upright rowing

Hold the bar with your arms straight down and your hands close enough together for the ends of the thumbs to be touching. Pull the bar up to the bottom of the chin, keeping the elbows high; pause for a few seconds before returning to the start position.

Upright rowing

Bent forward rowing

Bent forward rowing

Hold the bar with as wide a grip as possible while standing in a semi-crouched position. Keep the spine and arms straight, the knees slightly bent and the head looking forwards. Raise the bar to the chest by pulling the elbows high and to the sides of the body. Hold the bar against the chest for a few seconds before lowering slowly to the start position.

Press behind neck

Rest the bar in a comfortable position behind the head and across the shoulders, with the feet shoulder width apart. Press the bar above the head by straightening the arms. This is an exercise to strengthen the upper back muscles, and the weights should be raised without using the legs.

Trunk bend

Again rest the bar in a comfortable position behind the head and across the shoulders, with the feet shoulder width apart. Bend the knees to allow the body to reach forwards from the hips, keeping the spine straight and the head looking forwards.

Bench press

Lie on your back on a bench with the bar resting across the chest, the feet flat on the ground and the hands as wide apart as possible. Press the bar by straightening the arms and locking the elbows when the bar is at the highest point. Hold for a few seconds before lowering the bar slowly to the start position.

Single arm rowing

The feet are shoulder width apart with the legs slightly bent, and one hand rests on a bench to help to support the body weight. Keep the spine and the other arm straight, and hold the bar directly under the shoulder. Pull the bar to the side of the chest, keeping the elbow high; hold for a few seconds before lowering

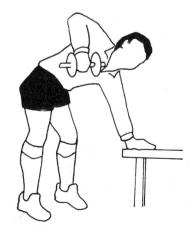

Single arm rowing

to the start position. Change hands after the set number of repetitions has been completed and repeat the exercise on the other side of the body.

Lateral raise

Stand with your feet shoulder width apart and the arms straight and relaxed, holding the weights at the lowest point. Raise the arms and weights out to the sides of the body, level with the ears. Keep the arms straight and hold this position for a few seconds before slowly lowering to rest the weights against the thighs.

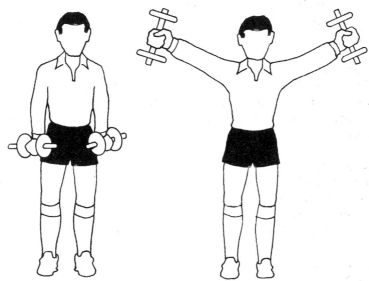

Lateral raises

Overhead pull

Lie on your back on a bench, with the feet flat on the ground and the bar held with straight arms above the chest (as in the bench press). Slowly lower the bar to a position behind and above the head, level with the body, keeping the arms straight at all times. Hold this position for a few seconds before returning to the start position.

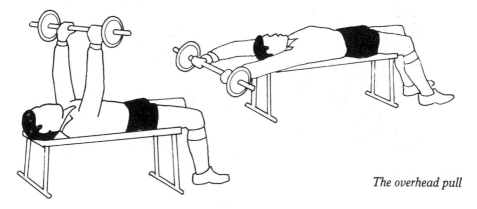

The overhead pull

The squat

Stand with the feet shoulder width apart and the bar held behind the head, resting comfortably across the shoulders. Slowly bend the knees and squat down until the thighs are parallel to the ground and no further. Hold the position for a few seconds before straightening the legs and returning to the start position.

The squat

Pre-season training

Although coaches will have stressed the need to train during the close season and possibly will have distributed specific fitness schedules, there are no guarantees that players will have followed the programmes to maintain a general level of fitness. Therefore pre-season training must be a carefully prepared series of sessions that gradually extend the cardio-vascular system of the heart and lungs.

Those players who have rigidly adhered to their close-season fitness programmes will obviously start pre-season training with a great advantage. The coach needs to ensure that the contents of the pre-season sessions are structured to extend everyone, i.e. players at different levels of fitness. The coach must stress to the players that training twice a week is insufficient to achieve the fitness levels needed to maintain an effective contribution for the duration of all of the games played during a season.

As well as attending club training nights and squad coaching sessions, players need to train individually, in pairs or in small groups, depending on personal circumstances. To encourage the players to achieve greater levels of fitness, the coach can advertise weekly training schedules on display boards. Hopefully this action could persuade some reluctant players of the values of extra training, particularly if the achievements of the fitter players are high-lighted as role models.

For the motivated players, weekly programmes will also ensure that the exercises they are doing are relevant to the general fitness needs of their particular playing unit. In all sports, players are always prepared to work at the exercises and skills in which they are competent. Few players willingly participate in activities in which they consider themselves to be weak, preferring to concentrate on the exercises in which they excel. By structuring two different training schedules, one suitable for forwards and the other for the three-quarters, the coach can include specific exercises to meet the demands of the distinct requirements of each playing unit.

Sample daily pre-season rotational training programme for a back-row forward

1 Establish target times for runs of varying distances, e.g.:

1.5 km (1 mile) in approximately 6 minutes

5 km (3 miles) in approximately 19 minutes

2 Sprints: 10×100 metres/yards in 14 seconds

(a) Initially walk slowly back to the starting point during the recovery period.
(b) Reduce the available recovery time by walking briskly back to the starting point.
(c) Further reduce the recovery period by jogging back to the start.

3 Exercises: complete the following series of exercises, continually rotating the order to concentrate the work on each part of the body in sequence – arms/trunk/legs.

(a) Pull-ups pyramid – overarm/underarm: 5:4:3:2:1, then 1:2:3:4:5. Aim to complete a pyramid of seven pull-ups both ways, increasing to a pyramid of ten repetitions if possible.
(b) 20 squat thrusts or burpees.
(c) 20 press-ups of various kinds (normal, wide-arm, and body inclined – both ways).
(d) 20 sit-ups of various kinds (normal, including twist, and body inclined both ways).
(e) 20 back arches of various kinds (normal, and hyper-extended dorsal raises lying on a bench).
(f) 2×20 step-ups (20 with each foot leading).
(g) If multi-gym available: wide arm bench press, pulling down weights.

Increase the workload by attempting to complete the circuit of exercises twice and then three times. Reduce the allowed recovery period between each exercise and attempt to complete three repetitions of the circuit in a particular time. Increase the number of repetitions of the most difficult and demanding exercises.

Day 1 Run 5 km (3 miles) in less than 19 minutes.
Day 2 Complete two repetitions of the exercise schedule.
Day 3 Run 1.5 km (1 mile) in less than 6.5 minutes.
Day 4 Sprint session.
Day 5 Rest.
Day 6 Run 1.5 km (1 mile) in less than 6.5 minutes and complete one repetition of the exercises.
Day 7 Have a sprint session and run 1.5 km (1 mile) in less than 6.5 minutes.

Continue to vary the combinations to make the training progressively more demanding until it is possible to complete the following schedule:

Day 1 Sprinting session: 10×50 metres/yards in less than 6 seconds and run 1.5 km (1 mile) in under 5.5 minutes.
Day 2 Run 5 km (3 miles) in less than 18 minutes, plus two repetitions of the exercises.
Day 3 Run 1.5 km (1 mile) in 5.25 minutes plus four repetitions of the exercise schedule.
Day 4 Run 5 km (3 miles) in 17.5 minutes.
Day 5 Complete two of the following sprint pyramids, using the walk back to the starting point of each sprint as the rest period:
4×25 metres/yards
3×50 metres/yards
2×75 metres/yards
1×100 metres/yards.

Circuit training

This form of training provides the coach with the opportunity to structure a concentrated fitness session that includes a variety of demanding, exhausting exercises and improves the fitness and strength of the players. By completing a record sheet of personal achievements during these sessions, both coach and players can determine and assess fitness levels and areas of individual weakness. Sessions can be individually tailored to players' needs to improve their overall cardio-vascular fitness and the strength of particular muscle groups.

The coach can organise different sessions for use either outside on the playing field or inside the confined space of a sports hall or gymnasium. The composition and layout of the session can be altered according to the facilities available. By using the different equipment and features at each facility, the coach can structure sessions that are challenging and interesting for the participants.

Circuit training can accommodate a large number of players, working either individually or in pairs. The structure of the session is regulated by the size of area available, range of equipment and the number of players in attendance. When working in pairs, it is advisable from a control viewpoint that the resting player records the achievements of his partner, by counting and registering the number of exercises completed during the allocated time, preferably during one minute of intense effort.

To prevent unnecessary delays or execution of poor technique during the training session, the coach should demonstrate each exercise and explain the order of completion. Every player must be familiar with the demands and correct performance of each exercise included in the session, and should be aware of the direction of movement required to complete the circuit. By preparing a diagram of the layout and route/sequence of exercises, the coach will be able to prevent players from extending their rest period.

It is important that the coach carefully controls the session to ensure that players rest only for the maximum period of one minute between each exercise. Regularly informing the players of the elapsed time during the exercises and the resting periods will ensure that everyone participates for the full minute. If players are working alone, the rest period must be used productively to record achievements, progress to the next exercise and move into position to commence it, while recovering from the previous exertions. Players working with a partner will be able to relax more between exercises, but they must not extend the rest period for any reason.

When planning the circuit, the coach must be careful to avoid a repetition in direct sequence of exercises that work the same muscle groups. The exercises must be alternated so that they work the larger muscle groups in the following order: arms, shoulders and upper body; abdominal area of the stomach and lower back; legs.

The illustrated structure and layout is for an indoor circuit, which can be altered to include different exercises or substitute activities to take advantage of the range of facilities available.

Training during the season

The only means of in-season training that provides players with the opportunity to rehearse, practise and improve their fitness, technique and skill is active participation in game-related practices, supplemented with endurance running and explosive exercises.

Working with the ball will always motivate players and result in greater commitment and involvement in the sessions. However, although game-related practices with the ball prove enjoyable for those involved, some players do not extend or involve themselves in large group practices as much as they should, often feigning injury or forwarding an excuse for their lack of commitment to the activity. Such lapses of application to the sessions, for any reason, will always prove detrimental to the fitness and performance of those players.

When introducing new practices to improve players' techniques it is necessary to perform the practices slowly so that the players can appreciate the demands and understand the key features. Occasionally it is necessary and justifiable to allow players to escape from the demands of a practice, perhaps to reduce the level of tension caused by the frustration and embarrassment of continual failure. To accommodate for the lack of fitness work during these learning periods and to ensure that any lapses of effort during the practices are not detrimental to the players' fitness levels, it is necessary to include a varied selection of endurance and speed work in each session.

During each training session it is valuable at some point for all of the players to work together in a large group and to participate in a range of different activities that concentrates on the improvement of fitness, team spirit and harmony. The coach should structure the content of these activities so that it is possible to record the results of each player's achievements, and thereby to add an extra dimension of competitiveness to the sessions. The fact that personal records are published and open to scrutiny by team-mates and other players who are competing for selection will ensure a high level of determination and commitment during training. It is only human for players to compare the achievements and results of others with their own, creating a competitive club atmosphere that will hopefully result in all of the players achieving greater levels of fitness and improved standards of performance.

However, the coach must monitor the effects of the record keeping on all of the players to make sure that it has a positive effect on individual self-esteem, levels of fitness and team spirit. It is important that the players take training seriously but do not become obsessed or paranoid about their achievements. Comments, comparisons and judgements of players by other players and the coaching staff during and after training should be aimed at encouraging friendly rivalry. It is important to keep the dialogue and rapport light hearted, helping to increase the levels of motivation and thereby to improve personal performances during coaching and training sessions.

It is also very important for the coach to avoid a regular routine for each training session. Players are not always enthusiastic about participation in rigorous training regimes or programmes. Everyone knows that it is foolhardy to attempt to participate in any sport unless in good health and physically fit, particularly in rugby football with its extra demands arising from body contact. However, players will attempt to avoid the more strenuous parts of each practice session if at all possible. If coaches always cover the fitness content early in each session, some players will arrive late with a convenient excuse that they were delayed by other commitments, managing successfully to avoid the endurance elements of the session. Including the specific fitness work in the middle or at the end of each session, when everyone is present, will prove more beneficial as well as more agreeable to the players who are always punctual.

Exercises for endurance training

Indian file running

Each player selects a partner of equal size, weight and speed to work with. They jog alongside one another, creating two straight lines of players running about a metre or yard apart. On the coach's instruction, the two players at the back of each line sprint to the front of their respective lines, with the coach awarding a point to the winner of each race. This running can be continued around the perimeter of the training ground or until one team scores a designated number of points.

As a penalty for their lack of success, the players on the losing team must complete a series of exercises of at least ten repetitions. These exercises should be varied, and should be completed correctly and quickly, with the coach further penalising the slowest player to complete the set number of repetitions. At suitable stages the coach can stop the running to include a range of exercises that can be done while working with and against a partner.

Scrummaging

The players scrummage against one another, each attempting to drive his partner backwards. On the coach's signal, the players must sprint 20 metres/yards to lines that have previously been highlighted with markers. After completing a set number of one exercise, for example ten squat thrusts, the players return to the centre of the area to resume scrummaging against their partner. It is important to vary the time that the players spend scrummaging (up to a maximum of 40 seconds).

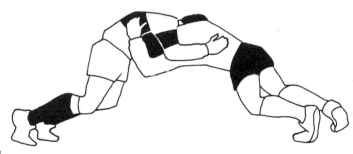

Scrummaging

Leg raise

One player lies on his back with his head against the feet of his partner and holds on to the ankles of his partner, who remains standing. The player on the ground keeps his legs together, with the toes pointed, and lifts them up towards his partner. When the feet reach the midriff of his partner they are pushed away at varying angles. The player raising his legs must prevent his feet from touching the ground before raising them again towards his partner. Twenty repetitions of this exercise are completed before the players change places.

Driving partner backwards

One partner acts as a resistance, attempting to prevent his partner from driving forwards. The player who is attempting to advance needs to assume a scrummaging position, making contact with his shoulder in his partner's midriff area. His head should be to the side of his partner and looking forwards in the direction of the intended finish of the exercise, ensuring that his back is kept straight.

Driving a partner backwards

Inclined press-up

Both players assume the press-up position before one inclines his legs by placing both feet in the centre of his partner's back. Both players complete ten press-ups at the same time before changing position.

Squats

Standing with his feet shoulder width apart and keeping a straight back, one player lifts his partner into a sitting position on his shoulders. To maintain good balance, he must hold the legs of the raised partner. Each support player completes ten squats, bending his legs until his thighs are parallel with the ground. It is important for him to pause for a few seconds in this squat position before standing upright again.

Partner as an obstacle

One player stands with his legs as wide apart as possible and his upper body leaning forwards. The other player leap frogs over his back and returns to the start position by crawling through the player's legs. Twenty repetitions are completed before they change places.

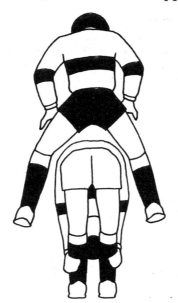

A partner as an obstacle

Wrestling

1 Two players wrestle with each other, each attempting to raise both of his partner's feet off the ground and win a point. The partner with the lower score when the coach stops the contest and all players who have tied scores are penalised and must complete a set of nominated exercises.

Wrestling

2 Two players sit back to back and link their arms. On the coach's instruction of left or right, each player attempts to pull his partner's upper body towards the ground on the side indicated by the coach. As before, a point is awarded to the victor and the loser completes a set of nominated exercises.

Back arch

Two players stand back to back with their feet shoulder width apart and arms linked. One player raises the other on to his arched back. While in this supported position the lifted player must follow the coach's instructions concerning leg movements, to work the stomach and thigh muscles – for example, keeping his legs together, crossing them over and doing horizontal cycling.

Partner as a counterweight

Two players squat back to back with their legs bent at the knees, feet on the ground and arms linked. They push against one another to counter their weight to allow each to move to a standing position. They return to the squatting position at the conclusion of each successful attempt. At least ten repetitions of this exercise are completed.

A partner as a counterweight

Sprinting

Sprint work on different terrain, including sand, gravel and hills, will considerably help to improve stamina and leg strength.

1 Partners sprint against the clock and one another over various distances.
2 Players work in groups according to the position that they play. For example: Gp 1, wingers and full-backs; Gp 2, centre three-quarters; Gp 3, half-backs; Gp 4, back-row forwards; Gp 5, second-row forwards; Gp 6, front-row forwards. Each group starts their run in a corner of the pitch; they sprint to the 22-m (25 yard) line and then complete a rectangle to finish at the original start point. The coach should time these runs, with each group starting at ten-second intervals. The circuit is completed three times before the distance of the run is extended to the half-way line and the intervals between the groups are increased to 20 seconds.
3 One player is selected from each group of forwards and three-quarters. Starting in the corner of the pitch, all of the players have to sprint diagonally across it from corner to corner; the two selected players are given a start of ten metres. For every player who overtakes the one given the head start, that player has to complete five exercises as a 'punishment'.

Organisation of practices

Functional practices that involve all of the players require detailed planning and organisation to make full use of the time, equipment and space available. This section provides some examples of game-related practices that can be incorporated into each session to develop the range of skills that are required in the various playing positions in rugby football. However, all coaches must be careful to ensure that the limitations and conditions imposed on players are relevant to their abilities and particular stages of development.

The factors that regulate the coach in planning the contents of each training session are:

1 the amount of usable space
2 the quantity and type of the equipment available
3 the number of players in attendance.

The practice area

Some clubs are fortunate enough to have access to more than one playing pitch or a training area that they can use throughout the year. If there is only a small training area available, it is a good idea to have coaching grids marked on the ground as near as practicable to the pitch.

The coaching grid

The coaching grid is a designated area of squares, each measuring 10×10 metres/yards that are marked on the training ground. A permanently available coaching grid measuring 60×40 metres/yards (24 squares) would prove a great asset and valuable resource. Within this limited area the coach can accommodate large numbers of players in concentrated practices, involving specific technical skill acquisition and development, or the rehearsal of tactical plays.

Restriction of players' efforts to a confined area helps to develop greater awareness of the problems that will be encountered during a game situation. Lack of time and space are the limiting factors that require players to select and execute the correct option with speed and efficiency. The creation of realistic, isolated situations in the practice area of the grids, which limit time and space, helps to prepare players for their participation in a competitive game.

Equipment

The content and method of each coaching and training session are limited by the quantity and diversity of the equipment available. Coaches should always ensure that a good supply of rugby balls is available. The game involves running and handling, making familiarity with the ball of paramount importance; consequently all practices should involve as much work as possible with the ball.

Other valuable equipment that can benefit the learning and development of the players includes:

1 a scrummaging machine
2 tackling bags
3 soft plastic fluorescent cones
4 posts and flags to use as markers
5 free-standing weights or a multi-gym; as these are large and expensive items to accommodate and purchase, it may be more suitable and cost-efficient to make arrangements to hire a sports hall that has these facilities available
6 training shirts and identification vests of two different light colours
7 old tyres or large hoops
8 first-aid kit
9 pump and a selection of different adaptors
10 large board to use as a visual aid for explaining tactical moves and training practices.

Acquisition of the basic skills

Every player can improve his level of performance in any sport; all that is required is determination and participation in an organised training programme, incorporating technical and skill development. All players participating in rugby training must be highly motivated and possess the dedication and perseverance to complete the demands of each practice as well as they can, to help them to realise their playing potential. When involved in skill development practices during training sessions, every player must concentrate on listening carefully to the instructions, comments and criticisms of the coach and other players to benefit from their expertise and experience.

Contained in this section are training practices that will help coaches to organise and improve the content and structure of their sessions. Active participation in these types of practices will improve the player's familiarity with the many different situations that he will confront during a game and positively influence his decision-making abilities to select the most appropriate action, after quickly assessing the positional developments at that particular moment. With constant encouragement, guile and the controlled introduction of pressure into the practices at the correct stage in the player's development, the coach will succeed in extending his repertoire of skills to enhance performance.

Unfortunately many coaches do not plan to include technical practices in training during the playing season, confining players' skill development to the pre-season sessions. For differing reasons many coaches prefer to concentrate on general fitness work, unit skills and team tactical practices. However, technical practices will result in higher standards of unit and team performances, as well as an improvement in players' basic skills and specific fitness levels.

All techniques and skills need to be rehearsed and practised in a training situation, where mistakes can be rectified by the coach and not punished by an opponent. The contents of sessions must be carefully structured and disciplined by the coach to improve the confidence and technical expertise of the players. This section will enable coaches to organise training sessions to include practices that concentrate on the acquisition of techniques particular to the needs of players, extending their working knowledge and understanding of the game and consequently improving their range of skills and overall playing standards.

The following practices attempt to cover the range of basic techniques that all rugby players should acquire. Within each practice is a section on the relevant coaching points, highlighting the key features, and there are suggestions on how to develop each practice. The coach must carefully consider when the players would benefit most from these progressions.

Passing

There are many different techniques and methods of transferring possession of the ball from one player to another. Each technique can be learned and practised in training, with the coach varying the conditions to increase the degree of pressure, reducing the amount of time and space that each player has available to execute a pass. During pressure practices a player may devise and demonstrate an individual or manufactured pass. Coaches should encourage individual flair and creativity, providing the results are effective and consistently successful. The basic techniques of passing should be practised regularly during training to develop confidence and expertise.

Although passing the ball laterally is probably considered to be one of rugby's most basic techniques and a particular feature of it, it is not the easiest of skills to demonstrate or execute. Because players are always seeking an opportunity to create or exploit space during the game, support players will require the ball to be passed towards them at different distances and angles. Running at speed with a ball is simple enough, but maintaining the forward momentum and passing the ball to the side and backwards, so that it can be easily caught by another player, is a very difficult manœuvre to control and perform accurately.

Types of pass

Dive pass
Although this technique can be seen as a specific pass used mainly by scrum-halves, all players need to be competent in its execution. Because of the transitional and flowing nature of the game, there are occasions when circumstances restrict the use of a preferred passing technique, or when a situation determines that another player must substitute for the scrum-half.

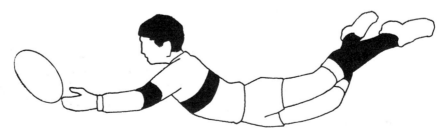

The dive pass

Spin pass

This pass is effective in passing the ball over long distances and is often favoured by the scrum-half to give the fly-half and three-quarters more time before they are pressurised by defenders. Because the ball spins laterally through the air, it travels quickly towards the receiving player, often making the catching of the ball difficult.

The spin pass

Switch or scissors pass

This pass is used to alter the direction of the attack, to wrong foot defenders and to keep the ball in play when the team is running out of space. Two players initially run parallel to one another. The ball carrier suddenly changes direction by running across and in front of the support player, turning towards the intended receiver, improving his view of the ball (while concealing it from the defenders), and giving a short pass.

Screen pass

This is a close interpassing skill that is used to transfer the ball over a short distance when committing an opponent to make a tackle to stop the forward-driving run of the ball carrier. The ball carrier must protect and control the ball by driving forwards and turning the shoulder into the defender, attempting to prevent the ball from being knocked to the ground. The proximity of the support players will affect the release of the ball which can be made:

1 slightly before contact is made with the defender
2 on the moment of impact with the opponent, or
3 after contact is made and behind the back of the tackler.

Loop pass

This is a slow and slightly arched pass given to the support player standing almost level with the ball carrier. Once the pass is given the inside player runs around behind the ball carrier to receive a short return pass, attempting to create an overlap situation or take advantage of a gap in the defensive line.

Flick pass

This is a quick method of passing the ball over a short distance when speed of

1

The switch/scissors pass

2

3

The screen pass

The flick pass

The reverse pass

transfer is vital. Rather than using the arms to swing across the body and fading the body away from the direction of the pass, this technique only uses the short movement of the wrists, which also allows the passer to retain his balance and continue running quickly to support the receiving player.

Reverse pass

This is used to alter the point of attack and to keep the ball in play. The ball is passed behind the back by either a spin or flick pass. It is common when:

1 the scrum-half is moving towards the touchline and the support is standing in a better position infield
2 attempting to deceive the opposition with moves that quickly alter the direction of attack, for example, the switch/scissors move.

Dummy pass

This is a deceptive movement that retains possession for the ball carrier after the execution of any one of the other techniques. At the normal point of release, the ball is pulled back into the body of the player to keep possession.

For all of the passing techniques there are several factors that will determine their effectiveness. It is possible to improve a player's ability to transfer the ball with regular practice in a variety of different situations and weather conditions. Different playing conditions will affect the selection of the method of passing and the technique will need to be slightly modified.

Each different situation will affect the selection of the appropriate technique, which will be influenced by the following criteria:

1 the length of the required pass
2 the speed of the advancing support player
3 the positioning of the defenders.

Key features of passing

1 The ball should be held in two hands at a comfortable height in front of the body.
2 The fingers are spread and relaxed to cover as much surface area of the ball as possible. This improves the security of possession and the control of the pass.
3 The hand behind the ball controls the direction and power of the pass.
4 The player should always look in the direction of the intended pass to assess the developing situation, including the positions of the support player, and make sure that the pass will not be intercepted by a defender.
5 The ball should be passed into the space slightly in front of the support player.

The dummy pass

6 The pass should be aimed at the receiver's midriff area, between the chest and hips, at a comfortable height to catch.

7 To conform with the laws of the game, the ball should always be passed backwards.

Exercise 1

Organisation
The exercise is carried out in groups of four, with each player standing in the corner of a 10 × 10 metre/yard grid. The players pass the ball to one another without moving from their position.

Coaching points
The ball is passed around the square in the direction determined by the coach. Change the direction of the passing regularly to help players to master passing the ball equally well to both sides of their body. Encourage the players to stand with their legs apart and to keep their feet in one position throughout the practice. Start this practice with the players facing into the grid.

Progression
1 Request the players to turn to face outwards, forcing them to turn their bodies through a greater range of movement.

2 When the players are competent at receiving and passing the ball in a stationary position, introduce movement into the practice. Once a player has received and passed the ball to the next player, he must follow the ball, running to the intended receiver's corner and then returning to his start point before the ball is passed around the square.

Exercise 2: familiarity with the ball

Organisation
Players work in small groups of three or four, with one ball in a 20 × 20 metre/yard grid area. The players move around passing the ball to one another without the ball falling to the ground.

Coaching points
Players must keep their eyes on the ball and be aware of its position at all times. Encourage them to reach for the ball to receive a pass, with their arms outstretched and their fingers spread as wide as possible and pointed towards the direction of the flighted pass.

Progression and further coaching points
Introduce competition by recording the number of successful passes completed

by each group in 30 seconds. Set players realistic targets and congratulate those who manage to accomplish them. Increase the intensity of the practice by introducing a defender to restrict the time and space that each player has available to receive and distribute the ball. Clearly identify the defending player by insisting that each one wears a different shirt or distinguishing vest. Do not allow any body contact or tackling at this point. The defender is successful and changes role with one of the other players when:

1 the ball is dropped to the ground
2 a player runs out of the grid in possession of the ball
3 the player with the ball is touched with two hands simultaneously, or
4 a pass by the attacking players is intercepted.

Restrict the players to passing the ball below shoulder height while moving around the grid area calling for the ball. Encourage players to swing their arms across the body to provide sufficient momentum to help to distribute the ball accurately and efficiently to another player.

Exercise 3

Organisation
Divide players into teams of at least three members each. The participants of each team line up in single file, with one ball between two teams, who stand facing each other across a 10×10 metre/yard grid area. The player in possession passes the ball to the first player in the team opposite and then sprints to the end of the receiving team's line. The receiving player catches the ball and returns a pass to the player opposite before following the ball and sprinting to the end of his line. Each player completes the practice as a relay shuttle.

Coaching points
The accuracy and weighting of the pass are the key factors in this practice. All players must keep their eyes on the ball, move in line with its flight and reach to catch the pass with outstretched arms and fingers. After catching the ball the players must hold it to the chest to secure possession while changing their standing position to a side-on stance. This helps them to generate the momentum of a controlled swing of the arms across the body to propel a pass efficiently and accurately in one movement.

Progression
Extend the distance between the teams and encourage the players to run with the ball in their hands to the half-way point of the grid area before passing to the player opposite.

Exercise 4

Organisation
Players form a circle around one player. The ball is passed from the player in the centre to a player standing in the circle; he returns it to the player in the centre, who then repeats the process with each player in turn.

Coaching points
Each player should have the opportunity to experience the concentrated period of passing and catching practice while standing in the centre of the circle. The weighting, speed and accuracy of each pass needs to be sympathetic to the position of the players to create a pressure practice situation for the player in the centre.

Progression
1 To increase the degree of difficulty, the players on the outside of the circle should run around the player in the centre. Change the direction of the running regularly.
2 Increase the size of the circle and introduce the condition that the player in the centre passes the ball to every player before a nominated player runs around the outside of the circle and returns to his starting point.
3 The introduction of a second ball for the more competent players further increases the pressure and tempo of the practice.

Exercise 5

Organisation
This is carried out by groups of three players with one ball in a 10 × 10 metre/yard grid area. The players pass the ball and move to another position in the grid to receive a return pass.

Coaching points
Start the practice with players in designated starting positions around the grid area. Encourage the players to experiment with different techniques of passing the ball, including the spin pass, dive pass and reverse pass. Players should communicate with one another, instructing the player in possession where to pass the ball.

Progression
1 Introduce a defender to attempt to intercept the passes, creating a 3 v. 1 situation. The defending player will limit the options available for the players in possession of the ball. This means that the support players must move around the outside of the grid to create different options and possible passing angles for

the player in possession. Change the defender regularly, because this is a physically demanding practice.

2 When the practice is proceeding successfully, introduce a second defender, creating a 3 v. 2 situation. If this restriction proves too difficult for the attacking players to achieve consistent success, introduce an extra attacking player to create a 4 v. 2 situation.

Exercise 6

Organisation
The players work in pairs in a large square, with one ball between each pair. The pairs move around the grid area passing the ball to each other, while at the same time avoiding contact with all of the other players.

Coaching points
Set high standards – do not accept inaccurate passing or poor technique. When a poor pass is made by a player, stop the practice to demonstrate good technique by swinging the arms across the body and allowing them to fall away from the direction of the pass. Highlight and acknowledge the players who are continually successful. Encourage players to keep their heads up to assess the continually developing situation in the grid, paying particular attention to the position of their partners.

Progression
Introduce one or two defenders into the grid to pressurise all of the other participants in the practice. Make sure that everyone can easily identify the defenders. Once a defender secures possession of a ball, he changes roles with the player from whom he acquired the ball.

Exercise 7

Organisation
Four players practise with one ball in a 20 × 10 metre/yard grid area. Each player stands on a corner of the designated area. The first player passes the ball along the 20-metre/yard line to the next player and runs after it. The second player passes the ball diagonally across the grid area and runs to the free position, changing places with the player who started the practice. The ball is then passed along the sideline to the fourth player, who continues the sequence of the practice.

Coaching points
This practice demands considerable concentration and effort. It is advisable to begin the practice slowly, carefully highlighting the organisation and demands

of the task. Be patient with the players until they fully understand the organisation. It is important that only the ball crosses the central area of the grid, with the players changing their position in pairs along the sidelines. Once the players have mastered the requirements of the practice, pressure can be introduced in a variety of ways, concerning the number of passes that can be completed in a given time, or the first team to complete a target number of passes.

Progression

Change the direction of the passing movement so that the ball is passed along the short side of the grid. It is important that the players listen attentively for the instructions of the coach. Introduce changes of direction and increase the pressure on the players by insisting that they complete a number of exercises before changing position. Make the changes and exercises both fun and demanding for the players. Do not attempt to progress to more challenging conditions until the players have mastered each change imposed on them.

Exercise 8

Organisation

A group of three has one ball in a 20 × 10 metre/yard grid area. Two players stand on a line of the grid with one positioned in the centre between the other players. The players are required to pass the ball to one another inside the grid as quickly as possible.

Coaching points

Set a target: each player should complete ten successful passes before another participant experiences the role in the centre of the grid, twisting and turning to receive the ball and complete a pass. The accuracy and the weighting of the pass are the key features in this practice. Encourage the players to pass the ball across both sides of their body, and discourage the player in the centre from continually turning in the same direction to receive and execute a pass.

Progression

1 Encourage the players to move up and down their respective lines as a small unit. Increase the speed of the running and the frequency of the passing.
2 Restrict the players to passing the ball only between the height of their waist and their knees.
3 Introduce a defender to pressurise the player in the centre of the grid. The defender's role must be clearly defined and monitored, with the player standing at the opposite end of the grid at the start of the practice. Initially restrict the defender to a passive role, attempting to catch the player in possession and prevent the passing movement from being completed.

Exercise 9

Organisation
Four attacking players are positioned around the outside of a 10 × 10 metre/ yard grid with two defending players inside the grid, creating a 4 v. 2 situation. The attacking players pass the ball to each other, while the two defenders attempt to intercept the passes. Any attacking player can move inside the grid area to support the player in possession, provided that the ball is passed immediately to one of the other attacking players standing outside the grid lines.

Coaching points
The defending players are not allowed outside the grid area; when the ball crosses the grid lines it is in the possession of the attacking players. Encourage players to keep their heads up to observe the changing positions of all of the players, allowing them to constantly assess the available options. The weighting, accuracy and control of the pass are the key features requiring particular attention. Set the attacking players the target of achieving ten consecutive passes, then change the roles of the players so that they share the experience of the defensive and attacking responsibilities. There should be continual movement of players around the grid area, attempting to create good passing angles to enable the player in possession of the ball to make a successful pass to another attacking player. Encourage the players to disguise their intentions, by feinting to pass the ball to one side of the defender but actually passing to a different player.

Progression
1 Extend the size of the grid to 40 × 20 metres/yards and insist that all players stay inside it. The attacking players' objective is to complete as many passes as possible before the two defenders force an error or intercept and secure possession of the ball.
2 Reduce the time and space available by increasing the number of participating players, creating 4 v. 3 or 5 v. 3 situations.

Exercise 10

Organisation
Six players create a 4 v. 2 situation in a 20 × 20 metre/yard grid area. One of the defenders has possession of a ball. Each group of players stands across the lines on the outside of the grid, facing one another. The defender starts by passing or kicking the ball to one of the four attacking players; their objective is to secure possession, pass the ball to one another and place the ball on the defenders' starting line before a defender intercepts a pass or causes a player to drop the ball and lose possession.

Coaching points

Insist on a good quality of service from the defenders; prevent them from advancing towards the attacking players until the ball has been caught. All of the players must commence the practice from their designated starting positions, ensuring that the space available to the attacking players is not limited by the defenders advancing too quickly. At the beginning, do not impose any conditions concerning the type or direction of the pass. A point is awarded to the attacking players each time the ball is placed on the ground behind the defenders' starting line. The defenders are awarded two points every time they intercept the ball and secure possession or cause the attacking players to drop the ball. Set a target of five points for either team to achieve before changing the roles of the attacking and defending players.

Progression

1 Restrict the height and technique with which the players are allowed to transfer the ball. The pass must be made using both hands and caught by a team-mate between the shoulders and the waist.
2 Introduce the condition that the ball can only be passed backwards.

Exercise 11

Organisation

Players work in groups of three with one ball in a 10 × 10 metre/yard grid area. One player starts in the centre of the end line of the grid; the other two players stand on either sideline at different distances away from the central player. He runs along the grid and the further player in possession passes the ball to the central support player, who must catch and pass the ball to the player standing on the other side of the grid before reaching the end line.

Coaching points

All of the passes must be accurate and correctly weighted. The players on the sidelines are stationary; only the player in the centre of the grid is moving. The players will need tremendous encouragement because it is a very difficult skill to run forwards and at the same time receive and distribute a lateral pass in a limited area. After a period of practice, start to penalise players with a set number of exercises if they pass the ball forwards. On reaching the end line the central player turns to repeat the practice. Change the positions of the players after five attempts have been successfully completed.

Progression

Once the players have mastered the skill of lateral passing, they can start in a line and run up and down the grid passing the ball.

Exercise 12

Organisation
Players work in groups of four with one ball in a 60 × 40 metre/yard grid area. The players run the length of the grid, continually passing the ball to one another.

Coaching points
The ball must always be passed backwards to conform with the laws of the game. Encourage players to pass the ball using different techniques, including one-handed, overhead and reverse passing. The players must run as straight as possible in suppport of one another, at varying distances and speeds. At the introduction of this practice it may be necessary to instruct the players to accelerate and include changes of speed in their running. Eventually it will prove more beneficial to make the players responsible for initiating their own changes of speed, testing the reactions and improving the responses of team-mates.

Progression
1 Insist that the players include particular movements during each run, for example: switch (scissors); loop; one-handed pass; overhead pass; a kick ahead; and missing a player with the pass.
2 Once the practice is progressing smoothly, attempt to break up the rhythm of the running by introducing different tasks that must be completed during the practice: for example, players must fall to the ground or complete a forward roll before getting to their feet and continuing.

Exercise 13

Organisation
Ten players with one ball create an 8 v. 2 situation in a 30 × 20 metre/yard grid area. None of the players is allowed into the central area of the grid. The attacking players on each side have to achieve a target number of passes between themselves before passing the ball to their team-mates on the other side of the grid. The defenders' role is to prevent the attacking players from achieving their target number of passes by attempting to intercept the passes and secure possession of the ball.

Coaching points
Encourage the support players to move around the grid to exploit the available space and to communicate with the ball carrier. Acknowledge good movement and highlight the occasions when players attract the defenders' attention and help to create an opportunity for the player in possession to successfully pass the ball to an unmarked player. The ball carrier can also create more space for

the pass by feinting a pass to a player standing on one side before passing to an unmarked player on the other side.

Progression
Introduce restrictions concerning the technique that should be used to pass the ball; regularly vary this condition to incorporate many different methods of passing the ball.

Switch passing

Organisation
Players work in pairs with one ball in a 20 × 10 metre/yard grid area. Each player starts the practice standing at opposite ends of the same line. The players run straight along the grid before the ball carrier changes the angle and direction of his run to accelerate towards the support player. This sudden movement is the cue for the support player to run behind the player in possession and receive a pass that changes the direction and point of the attack.

Switch passing

Coaching points
The effectiveness of this passing movement revolves around the elements of surprise and the speed of execution. The player in possession needs to give the impression that he intends to keep running straight before quickly changing speed and direction to alter the angle of the attack. The support player should never close the space between the two players until the ball carrier changes the angle of his run, helping to further deceive the defenders who are later introduced into the practice. The ball carrier must always be aware of the position

and the running angle of the support player. There are three different methods of transferring the ball to the support player:

1 a flick pass
2 a reverse pass, or
3 holding the ball at waist height for the other player to take and secure possession.

All of these techniques should be practised and mastered because each support player executing the switch move will prefer a different kind of pass. The exchange of the ball should occur in the centre of the grid.

Progression
1 Introduce a defender, creating a 2 v. 1 situation. Encourage the ball carrier to include a dummy switch, completing the same actions as before but retaining possession of the ball and using the run of the support player as a decoy to deceive the defender. Change the players' roles at regular intervals to allow everyone to attempt the execution of the switch and dummy switch pass.
2 Increase the number of players and the size of the grid area accordingly to create 3 v. 2 and 4 v. 3 situations, with the attacking team always maintaining a numerical advantage.

The loop pass

Organisation
Players work in groups of four with one ball in a 60 × 40 metre/yard grid area. The player in possession of the ball starts in one corner, with the other players in a line alongside. Running as straight as possible, the players pass the ball along the line. After making a pass each player runs to the outside position, looping around the other three players to keep the movement flowing.

Coaching points
Once the players have passed the ball they must run behind their team-mates to reach the outside of the line as quickly as possible. At the beginning, discourage players from transferring the ball as quickly as possible. This is essentially a passing practice that requires good support running; by encouraging the players to swing the ball smoothly and effectively across themselves and not to fall away with their bodies from the direction of the pass, they will become more effective in completing its demands. When he is supporting on the outside of the line, a player must run as straight as possible towards the end of the grid area and not towards the sidelines. If the players start their support run from a deeper position they will be better able to alter their running angle to make sure that they run straight.

The loop pass

Progression

1   The player starting the practice must loop around each player in sequence to receive a return pass and concentrate on keeping the line of players running straight to the end line of the grid. When the first player reaches the end of the line and catches the ball the players stop running, place the ball on the ground, assess their position and continue, with a different player starting the practice. It will possibly be necessary for the players to change the direction of their attack, as they may have used most of the grid space when completing this practice at speed.

2   For a variation on the means of transferring the ball, and to make sure that the looping player does enter the line of players running straight, insist that the receiving players do not pass the ball but hold it out level with their hip. The supporting player must take the ball from the player and drive forwards for a few metres/yards in a low, crouched position before passing to the next player and continuing the support running, looping each player in turn.

Screen Pass

Organisation

Players work in larger groups of five, six or seven with one ball in a 60×20 metre/yard grid area. This is a close interpassing practice that requires the players to keep the ball in play with intelligent support running.

Coaching points

To concentrate the attention of the players, give each member of the group a number to ensure that they complete the passing in sequence. The players must run as straight as possible, with the support player approaching the ball carrier from a deep position. Introduce the condition that either:

1 the support player determines which side the player in possession passes the ball, or
2 the ball carrier calls out which side the support player should run to receive the pass.

If the ball is dropped, possession should be secured as quickly as possible by the support player and the practice should be continued.

Progression

1 Vary the transfer of the ball to include different techniques of passing: flicks, one-handed and reverse passes, and the player in possession simply holding the ball for the support player to take.
2 The quality of the service should be varied to include passes at different heights.
3 Introduce defenders to attempt to disrupt the momentum and rhythm of the players.
4 Increase the size of the working area to provide the players with the opportunity of varying the distance of the passes and allow them to create and exploit better attacking positions.

Handling and running

Every player must be familiar with the ball and participate regularly in practices to learn the basic skills of handling, including catching and running with the ball, picking up and falling on the ball.

Each practice should create different and particular problems for the players to overcome and further their experience of a range of handling and running skills that are effective for all situations and weather conditions. Players have to be able to make decisions very quickly based on their assessment of the developing nature of the game, the state of play and their location on the field. The selection and performance of an appropriate handling technique or running

New Zealand's Wayne Shelford attempts to hand-off a determined Welsh challenger

action for a given situation can determine the outcome and result of a game. The most successful teams are those that contain individuals who are capable of a sound performance of the basic handling techniques, limiting the number of errors, to take advantage of scoring opportunities created by players driving forwards and elusive running skills.

Key features of handling

The factors affecting the selection of the correct technique to ensure the retention or acquisition of possession of the ball are:

1 the direction of flight of the ball
2 the combined momentum of the player and ball
3 the height of the ball
4 the movement of the ball, whether spinning, rolling or stationary
5 weather conditions.

Catching
1 Watch the ball through the entire duration of its flight from the moment of its release.
2 Manœuvre the body into a position that will help to secure possession and will also allow a smooth transfer into the next action.
3 Move the hands and body into line with the flight of the ball.
4 Turn the shoulders and upper body sideways towards the ball.
5 Reach towards the ball with the fingers relaxed and spread to present the largest reception area possible.
6 Gradually reduce the ball's speed by slowly withdrawing the hands on contact, cushioning the force and slowing down the momentum of the ball to secure possession.

The following techniques are methods of securing possession of the ball in the transitional periods of broken play. It is far easier to pick up a stationary ball than a moving one because of the unpredictability and variability of the movements of a rugby ball; the surer technique to secure possession is to fall on the ball.

Picking up
1 Keep watching the ball.
2 Stoop towards the ball in a low, crouched position, keeping the body balanced.
3 Place the foot of the rear leg behind the ball at a comfortable distance that allows the arms to swing through to the ball without being impeded.
4 The leading leg should be placed to the side and slightly beyond the position of the ball.
5 Hands should be placed either side of the ball with the fingers relaxed and spread as wide as possible.
6 The hand that is further away from the body pulls the ball upwards and towards the guiding hand.

Falling on the ball
1 Fall beyond the ball on to the side of the body, with the chest facing towards the ball.
2 Place the hands either side of the ball to secure possession, pulling it into the midriff area.
3 Stand up with the ball as quickly as possible, attempting to use the ground as a trampoline to bounce back on to the feet.

Running with the ball
1 Keep the ball secure, under control and in contact with one or both hands by spreading the fingers to cover the maximum surface area of the ball that the size of the hands allow.

2 Always run on the balls of the feet and lean the upper body weight slightly forwards to help to maintain momentum.

3 Vary the running speed, attempting to foil the efforts of an opponent.

4 Include a side-step or swerve to change direction and avoid the challenges of defenders.

Side-step: this is performed by transferring the body weight on to one leg and pushing against the ground to quickly change the direction of the run.

The swerve

Swerve: this is a smooth running action in which the legs and hips move in an arc out of reach of the defender. It is easier to perform this evasive action when carrying the ball against the body, freeing one arm to push away the tackling player.

Hand-off: either pushing away the defender, or pushing against the tackler to move the body out of reach and change the angle of running. To execute a good hand-off the ball carrier needs to make a good contact with the upper body of the tackling player.

The side-step

The hand-off

Catching a high ball

Organisation
Players work in pairs with one ball in a 30 × 10 metre/yard grid area. The players can either throw or kick the ball into the air for their partner to catch.

Catching a high ball

Coaching points
Insist that the players are accurate with the service of the ball, remaining inside the confines of the grid area. Players should keep their eyes on the ball at all times, concentrating their attention on its flight to assess the place of descent and moving to that position to make the catch. The arms should be raised close together towards the ball, keeping the palms of the hands and the fingers outstretched. This helps to create a large reception area for the ball in the shape of a cradle or basket with the arms and upper body. It is important to relax when making the catch to help the hands and fingers to cushion the force of the falling ball, guiding it into the chest with the arms curling around the ball. Players should also be encouraged to turn side on to the ball when making the catch, to prevent any handling errors that might result in the ball being knocked forwards.

Progression
1 Introduce a competitive element by insisting that the players complete five exercises when one of the following occurs:
(a) a poor service prevents the execution of the correct technique
(b) a player fails to catch a good service
(c) one player completes three good catches in a row.

2 Increase the pressure on the receiver by telling each server to assume the role of an opponent and advance towards the player when the ball is in the air.
3 One player assumes the role of defender and stands on the end line of the grid to serve the ball, staying on the line until the ball is caught. The other player has five attempts to catch the ball and reach the server's line to score a try before the defender touches him with two hands. This will prepare the player to constantly assess the situation, think ahead and plan his next move once he has possession of the ball.
4 Increase the degree of difficulty of the service to make the receiving player turn to catch the ball.
5 Increase the size of the grid and gradually introduce more players, creating a greater number of options for the player who is catching the ball. Encourage players to call for the ball when taking responsibility for a catch, giving the other players the opportunity to move into good support positions.

Picking up the ball

Organisation
Players work in teams of three with one ball in a 60 × 10 metre/yard grid area. The practice starts with the players running in single file; the first player has possession of the ball. The ball carrier runs to the first line and places the ball on to the line to score a try before moving to the side to allow the next player to pick up the ball. After the players score the try they move to the side and wait to join on to the end of their team to continue the practice.

Picking up a ball

Coaching points
When picking up the ball the players should always watch it, place their front foot to the side but in front of the ball, bend their knees and perform a scooping action with the hands, which are placed on the bottom half and either side of the ball. The fingers should be spread wide to cover the maximum possible surface area of the ball. Make sure during the early stages of the practice that the player scoring the try does so correctly and that the ball is stationary for the support

player to practise the pick up. Once the possession of the ball is secured, the ball carrier must accelerate for several metres/yards to add impetus to the practice.

Progression

1 Increase the degree of difficulty of the pick up by allowing the players to place the ball on the ground at any point.
2 Introduce competition in the form of relay races.
3 Insist that the ball carrier stoops to roll the ball forwards along the ground instead of scoring a try.
4 Alter the organisation so that two teams stand facing each other across a 30 × 10 metre/yard grid area and work in a relay practice with one ball. The ball carrier runs forwards to score a try in the last grid before sprinting to touch the first player of the other team and joining the end of their line. The player runs to pick up the ball, sprints forwards and also scores a try in the final grid. Set a target for the teams, for example to complete a particular number of repetitions.
5 One player assumes the role of server to the other players. The server stands with the ball, facing the line of players who are standing at the opposite end of the grid. The ball is rolled along the ground and must be picked up by a player; he runs to return it to the server, who continues the practice with each player in turn.

Falling on the ball

Organisation

Players work in pairs in a 10 × 10 metre/yard grid area, with the ball placed on the ground in the centre of the grid. The players take it in turns to secure possession by falling to the ground beside the ball and standing up as quickly as possible, holding the ball in two hands. After each successful attempt the ball is placed back on the ground and the player returns to the side of the grid to allow his partner the opportunity to practise the skill.

Coaching points

The position of the body is the most important factor. Make sure that the player keeps his eyes open and falls to the ground on his side beyond the ball but facing it. On making contact with the ground, he should curl the body around the ball, pull the chin towards the chest to protect the head, and wrap the arms around the ball to secure possession. When possible he should return immediately to a standing position, attempting to use the ground like a trampoline to bounce back on to the feet.

Progression

1 The ball is rolled along the ground inside the grid for the partner to fall on it.
2 One player assumes the role of attacker and dribbles the ball inside the grid

area, occasionally pushing it too far forwards and out of playing distance. This provides the opportunity for the defender to fall on the ball.

3 Extend the size of the grid to 30 × 10 metres/yards and place three balls on each line in front of each team of three players. Introduce competition in the form of relay races, with each player falling on all three balls in sequence before returning to the starting position, allowing the next player to complete the practice.

Elusive running (1)

Organisation
Groups of three or four stand in a straight line; the first player runs along a 60-metre/yard grid line, weaving in and out of the posts or cones that are placed at intervals on the line.

Coaching points
The distance between the posts or cones should be fairly large to start with. Encourage players to attempt both the side-step and body swerve, including combinations of both during their run. Do not be tempted to introduce competition too early; give the players every opportunity to experiment and perfect their evasive skills. When swerving, players must lean with their upper body towards the post, attempting to keep their feet and hips as far away as possible. The players can return to the start point by continuing to avoid the posts, or they can sprint back as quickly as possible by running alongside the grid line.

Progression
1 Stipulate that particular skills should be performed on certain runs.
2 Increase the frequency of the runs and introduce a competitive element; for example, as soon as the player in front reaches the first post, the next player can start his run.
3 Gradually reduce the distance between the posts.
4 Increase the number of posts.
5 Introduce a ball and insist that players always carry it in two hands.
6 Change the position of the posts so that they are no longer in a straight line, but randomly placed inside a 60 × 10 metre/yard grid area.
7 Make the practice competitive by running it as a relay race.

Elusive running (2)

Organisation
Players work in pairs with one ball in a 20 × 10 metre/yard grid area. One player assumes the role of attacker in possession of the ball, while the other attempts to mirror the movements of the ball carrier.

Coaching points

Players must keep their heads up to make sure that they remain within the confines of the grid area. Change the players' roles regularly to stimulate speed of thought and reduce the reaction time of both players. Encourage the players to demonstrate their complete repertoire of running skills in an attempt to lose their shadow. Pair together players of similar abilities, and avoid any mismatches.

Progression

1 The player in possession must keep as far away as possible from the defender, who attempts to catch the player by touching him with both hands.
2 The players stand at opposite ends of the grid, facing each other; the ball carrier is given five attempts to reach the other player's line without being caught, and is awarded a point for each successful attempt. The player in each grid with the least number of points must complete a set number of exercises as a penalty.
3 Alter the starting position of the defending player, first to the corner of the grid and then to the midway point along the sideline.

Elusive running (3)

Organisation

This is a shuttle relay practice with the players in teams of three or four in a 40 × 10 metre/yard grid area. Each team has one ball, which must be carried in two hands at all times. A number of marker cones are placed at varying intervals along the grid. The players must side-step or swerve in alternate directions past each cone, run to the 40-metre/yard line and return by the same route to pass the ball to the next member of the team.

Coaching points

Initially place the cones a fair distance apart until the players are familiar with the demands of the practice. Encourage players to use this practice to develop a range of running and handling skills.

Progression

1 Transfer the ball to the next player with a dive pass from inside the first grid.
2 Extend the distance of the run and bring the marker cones closer together.
3 Kick the ball along the ground or up in the air at the midpoint of the run and recover it before returning to the start.
4 Perform a dummy pass during the return run.

Elusive running (4)

Organisation

Players work in pairs with one ball in a 10 × 10 metre/yard grid area. One player assumes the role of attacker in possession of the ball, and the other acts as defender. The object of the practice is for the attacker to avoid the defender and reach a designated point to score a try.

Coaching points

Encourage players to include a feint, side-step or swerve as well as a change of pace to accelerate past the defender. The defender can prevent the attacker from achieving his objective by touching the attacker with two hands on the waist.

Kicking the ball

Every player needs to be competent in kicking the ball. The range of techniques required by each participant is primarily determined by his playing position, his interest and his success in performing the different techniques. The basic reasons for kicking the ball are:

1 starting and re-starting the game
2 gaining a better forward position
3 relieving pressure
4 changing the emphasis and point of the attack
5 scoring points for the team.

Kicking is affected by the weather conditions more than other aspects of playing, making the selection and execution of the correct technique vitally important. Therefore players who perform an important kicking role during a game must practise all of the different techniques on a regular basis.

Key features of kicking

1 The objective of the kick will affect the selection of technique, except at re-starts when players must conform to the laws of the game.
2 Establish a routine of concentrating exclusively on the execution of the action.
3 The non-kicking foot should provide a sound base to support the body weight and should work in conjunction with the arms to help to control balance.
4 The speed of the kicking leg determines the power generated by the foot on the ball.
5 The point of contact must be along the longitudinal centre line of the ball.
6 The knee should be over the ball at the point of contact.
7 The head should be still, with the player concentrating on the ball from the beginning of the approach to the conclusion of the action.
8 The kicking leg should follow through after the ball and finish with the foot pointing in the intended direction of the kick.

Gavin Hastings of Scotland meticulously prepares for a kick at goal

Kicking the ball out of the hands – the punt

Organisation
Players work in pairs and stand about five metres/yards apart, facing one another with one ball in a 10 × 10 metre/yard grid area. Holding the ball in two hands, they practise kicking the ball accurately to one another.

Coaching points
Place one hand at each end of the ball and hold it at waist height at a comfortable distance in front of the body, with the arms relaxed. The ball should point down towards the non-kicking foot. Keep the head still and eyes on the ball. Turn the body slightly to one side to allow the kicking leg to swing through to the ball, which is dropped carefully on to the foot. Strike through the middle of the ball, concentrating on accuracy rather than power, with an extended ankle and the toes pointing towards the ground. Keep the head and knee over the ball, leaning backwards on contact with the ball. The non-kicking foot must provide a firm base to help the player to maintain balance, and it must point in the direction of the intended path of the ball. The lower leg must continue to follow

The punt

through after striking the ball to finish with the foot pointing towards the intended target. Encourage players to alternate the use of each leg to execute the skill.

Progression

1 Set a target for the players to complete before increasing the distance between them.
2 Move to the side of the grid to practise kicking the ball along the lines.

The drop kick

Organisation

Players work in pairs with one ball in a 40 × 10 metre/yard grid area. Each player drops the ball to hit the ground before kicking it in the direction of his partner.

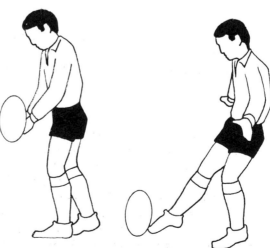

The drop kick

Coaching points

The ball must be held upright at waist height with the hands placed on either side. It may be necessary for the players to first practise dropping the ball to the ground in front of them to land on its point, leaning slightly towards them. This will result in the ball bouncing upwards and backwards, increasing the contact area for the foot to kick the ball. Contact should be made with either the toe or laces of the boot on the lower third of the ball. The head must be kept still and the eyes on the ball. At the moment of contact the upper body should be relaxed and leaning backwards to help to achieve height with the kick, and the lower leg should follow through in the direction of the intended target. The ankle should be kept firm when the player drops the ball directly in front of the body and the ball is struck with the front of the foot. With a rotational approach, when the ball is dropped in front and slightly to the side of the body to allow for greater leg speed, the ankle should be kept extended to strike the ball with the laces/bridge of the foot. Move the arms out to the side of the body to help to maintain balance.

Progression

1 Award a point to the player who drop kicks the ball over his partner's head inside the 22-metre (25-yard) line and give the players a set number of attempts to try to drop kick the ball between the posts and score a point. The player with the least number of successful attempts must complete a number of exercises.
2 Include a defender who moves towards the kicker to add more pressure.
3 Players must pick the ball off the ground and then attempt a drop kick at goal.
4 The ball is passed to the player and caught before the drop kick can be attempted.

Kicking the ball along the ground – the grubber kick

Organisation

Players work in pairs, standing 20 metres/yards apart and facing one another in the centre of a 40 × 10 metre/yard grid area. They practise kicking the ball along the ground, attempting to make the reception and catching of the ball as difficult as possible for the partner.

Coaching points

Use the partner as the target of the intended kick. Keep the head still and the eyes looking at the ball during the execution of the technique. The ball needs to be dropped carefully on to the larger surfaces of the foot to ensure control and accuracy. The head and the knee of the kicking foot should move over the ball to ensure a good contact. Strike through the centre of the ball with the non-kicking foot placed to the side of the body to improve balance and pointing in the direction of the target. After making contact with the ball, swing the leg to follow through in the direction of the intended path of the ball.

The grubber kick

Progression
1 Gradually increase the distance between players.
2 Alternate the service by using only one hand to drop the ball.
3 Limit a particular number of attempts to kick the ball to the use of either the left or the right foot.
4 Drop the ball at different places in front of the body to continually alter the contact point.
5 Limit the number of times the ball can bounce on the ground between the players. This will force the players to consider and attempt a range of different kicking techniques that alter the point of contact of the foot on the ball to determine where the ball first hits the ground.
6 When the players are 40 metres/yards apart, introduce competition by awarding a point to the player who succeeds in kicking the ball past his partner and beyond the end line of the grid. When one player has scored three points, he moves to the grid on his right-hand side to challenge a different player.

Place kicking

Organisation
This is a concentrated practice intended only for the small group of players who are responsible for the re-starts in the game and for taking the goal kicks. To rehearse their techniques, either an angled or straight approach, the players can work in pairs along a line of a grid, before progressing to attempt to kick the ball through the goal posts from a variety of angles and distances.

The angled approach: this is the most common technique because the ball is struck with a large surface area on the bridge/laces of the foot. On contact the toes point towards the ground, with the ankle extended.

The well balanced body position and high follow through of New Zealand's Grant Fox will enable him to achieve both accuracy and distance in his goal kicking

The straight approach: the player stands behind the ball to create a straight line to the posts. The ball is kicked with the smaller surface area of the toe, with the ankle flexed at the point of contact.

Place kicking – angled approach   *Place kicking – straight approach*

Coaching points

Players should experiment with both techniques, deciding for themselves which is the more suitable and successful and place the ball carefully on the ground so that the point of contact is clearly visible; players may prefer individual styles of positioning the ball, such as pointing towards the posts, angled towards the kicker or sitting upright. The manner of preparing the ground for the ball will be decided by the position of the ball.

The approach towards the ball must be appropriate for the style of kicking and consistent for each attempt. The non-kicking foot should be placed onto the side of the ball, pointing in the direction of the intended flight and at a distance that provides a stable base, good balance and allows the kicking foot to swing freely and follow through after contact. It is important to keep the head still with the eyes on the ball and to relax by taking a deep breath. As the non-kicking foot is placed beside the ball, throw the arms out to the side of the body to help to maintain good balance. The players will need a good supply of balls to maximise the use of the time and complete a number of attempts before changing their roles, attempting to develop a successful and consistent style and rhythm. The concentrated nature of this type of practice means that any technical faults can be observed, discussed and corrected immediately.

The short chip kick (1)

Organisation

Players work in pairs with one ball in a 30 × 10 metre/yard area. They chip kick the ball from one end zone to the other, avoiding the central grid area.

Coaching points

Clearly mark the central zone by placing cones in the corners. The ball must be carefully dropped on to the foot, which swings through more slowly than for the other kicks. The ankle should be flexed, with the toes pointing forwards and upwards in the direction of the intended flight of the ball. The key feature is the weighting of the contact of the ball with the foot, which is determined by the

The short chip kick

speed of the lower part of the leg moving towards the ball. The knee of the kicking leg must be kept high, with the head still, eyes on the ball and the body leaning backwards at the moment of impact of the foot and the ball. The non-kicking foot should provide a solid base and help to maintain good balance. Encourage players to use both their left and right foot and not to favour one foot all of the time.

Progression

Introduce a competitive element by awarding points to the kicking player when his partner fails to catch the ball or it hits the ground inside the target grid. After a couple of minutes stop the practice and move the more successful players into the next grid area on the right. The most accomplished players will eventually compete against one another in the end grid, improving the intensity of the practice.

The short chip kick (2)

Organisation

Players work in teams of three in a 30 × 10 metre/yard grid area with one ball. The participants line up one behind the other in their teams and stand at opposite ends of the grid, facing one another. The ball carrier runs towards the other team and performs a chip kick in the central area of the grid; he then attempts to catch the ball before it hits the ground, or he recovers possession as quickly as possible. He then continues towards the first player in the opposite team and passes the ball for the practice to be continued as a shuttle relay. On completing the task, each player moves to the end of the line and awaits further attempts.

Coaching points

The key feature of the practice is the player's ability to control the weight and accuracy of the chip kick. He should carry the ball in two hands and make an early decision on the choice of the kicking foot. The ball should be dropped carefully into the space in front of the body to avoid the knees, allowing the kicking foot the opportunity to swing through to strike the ball. Before attempting the chip kick the player must be well balanced, with the head still and the eyes on the ball. After kicking the ball, he must quickly assess its flight to determine the landing area and catch the ball before it hits the ground. When the ball is kicked too far forwards, making the catch difficult or perhaps impossible before the ball hits the ground, the chasing player must pick up the ball and secure possession as quickly as possible.

Progression

Increase the pressure on the players by introducing a defender (the first player in the line opposite) into the practice. Both players move forwards at the same time and the player in possession must chip the ball over the advancing player.

The kick over the shoulder

Organisation

Although all players should learn this kick, it is the scrum-halves, wingers and full-backs who will need to be involved in the more concentrated periods of pressure training. The players work in pairs and stand facing one another in a 30×10 metre/yard grid area with one ball. One player stands on the end line of the grid in possession of the ball and assumes the role of server: the other player is 20 metres/yards away. The ball is thrown or kicked (depending on the ability of the server) accurately over the head of the receiving player, who must turn to catch it. Once possession is secured the player must immediately kick the ball over his shoulder, attempting to return it to the server.

Coaching points

A good-quality service is vital to allow the player to turn and catch the ball easily. The receiving player must carefully observe the flight of the ball. Insist at the beginning of the practice that the ball is kicked back over one particular shoulder for a designated number of attempts before the players change roles. After securing possession the receiving player will need to slightly rotate his hips and lean backwards, allowing the kicking foot to freely swing through to make contact with the ball. He should strike the ball with the bridge of the foot and follow through with the lower leg. The non-kicking foot should provide a good base to support the body weight and help to maintain balance until the ball is kicked. It is likely at the early stages that the receiving player will fall to the ground after kicking the ball as a result of leaning backwards during the execution of the technique; therefore do not operate this practice on hard ground or during miserable weather conditions.

Progression

1 Players will always favour their stronger kicking foot, so encourage the use of the weaker foot.
2 Develop the role of the server to act as defender once the ball is played accurately to the receiving player.

Dribbling the ball

Organisation

Divide the squad into small teams of three or four players. The teams stand in single file, one behind the other along the same line, with a ball placed on the ground ten metres/yards in front of each team. In turn the players must run to the ball and dribble it along the ground to a designated marker. On reaching the marker they must pick up the ball, run with it to the starting position and score a try, before touching the next player to continue the practice as a relay.

Coaching points

Keep the eyes on the ball, looking up occasionally to check on the direction of the run and the position of the target line. Place the arms out to the side to help to maintain good balance. Use the larger surfaces of the instep and outside of the foot to kick the ball. Always keep the ball within playing distance, under control and close to the feet. Use both feet to dribble the ball. The emphasis should be on keeping the ball moving forwards under control. Inform the players about the number of successful runs required to complete the relay.

Progression

1 Restrict contact with the ball to one particular foot.
2 Use only a nominated part of one foot.
3 Include different sequences of movements after possession of the ball is secured; players are required to perform difficult skills with the ball in their hands, for example, dummy pass, side-step, swerve, chip kick and catch.

Kicking game

Organisation

This game is played in a 60 × 40 metre/yard grid area. It involves twelve players in a 6 v. 6 situation with one ball, or all of the players divided into two equal teams in a larger section of the playing area, for example, playing across the pitch between the two 22-metre (25-yard) lines. The players practise kicking the ball backwards and forwards across the centre line or a designated area, and points are awarded to the kicking team every time the ball hits the ground before the receiving players catch it.

Coaching points

Place cones to identify the centre line or zone that must be cleared by the ball and avoided by the players. Encourage the players to announce that they are taking responsibility to catch a particular ball. The players are allowed to kick the ball to a team-mate but risk the loss of points should the kick be inaccurate or dropped to the ground. Limit the number of kicks before the ball must be returned across to the other team. Differentiate between the techniques used, awarding one point for a punt or chip kick, two points for a drop kick and three points for a place kick. Inform the players at the beginning that points are not deducted if the ball hits the ground when they attempt a drop kick or place kick. Set a target of ten points for each game, with the condition that the winning team must be two clear points ahead of their opponents.

Progression

1 Introduce a second ball to increase the tempo and intensity of the game.
2 Change the scoring system so that teams can only be awarded points if
(a) they execute a particular technique, or
(b) the ball hits the ground in certain designated areas marked with cones.

Tackling

Although tackling is a very important aspect of the game and a skill that can be improved with training and practice, it is often neglected by coaches. The most likely reason for this is the risk of injury to players during tackling practices. This risk can be reduced by good organisation, careful planning and strict control of the sessions.

For periods of extensive technical practice, tackling bags can be invaluable to improve players' confidence and develop their repertoire of skills. To consolidate their learning, players must also participate with other players in controlled and realistic practice situations that involve tackling and being tackled. Both of these training methods must be used to complement one another, to perfect the techniques of tackling and prepare players for the direct physical confrontations and challenges that occur during a game of rugby football.

The successful execution of a good tackle can significantly alter the balance of a game; for example, a good tackle could prevent a player from advancing beyond the gain line or scoring a try, helping to create an opportunity to turn defence into attack.

Key features of tackling

1 Assume a good position and try to manœuvre the ball carrier into a situation in which his options are limited, attempting to gain the initiative to determine and predict the actions of the attacker.
2 Keep the eyes open.
3 Generate as much force into the tackle as possible by driving into the ball carrier from a good base, launching the body to make a solid contact with the shoulder either just above the knees or in the midriff area.
4 Wrap the arms around the opponent's body or legs to establish a firm grip to unbalance the ball carrier and force him to the ground.
5 Position the head to the ball carrier's side in a safe place.
6 Attempt to gain and secure possession of the ball if possible.

The key features of tackling

Developing tackling power (1)

Organisation

Players work in small groups and begin by kneeling down in straight lines facing the tackling bags. This practice can take place either inside (in a sports hall or gymnasium with the added use of mats) or outside in small grids. The players drive into the tackling bag to develop the confidence needed to tackle.

Coaching points

The eyes must be kept open and fixed on the intended point of contact of the shoulder with the tackling bag. Drive the body forwards by straightening the legs to provide power. Place the head to the side of the bag on contact in a safe position. Move the arms forwards, wrap them around either side of the bag and pull towards the body. This wrestling action of the arms, combined with the forward drive of the shoulder and upper body, will result in the bag falling to the ground. The players take turns to perform the tackle, moving to the back of the line after each attempt. This organisation can be used to teach the technique of tackling from the front and from the side. Make sure that everyone is tackling from the same direction and executing the same technique to avoid any mishaps caused by bags colliding against one another.

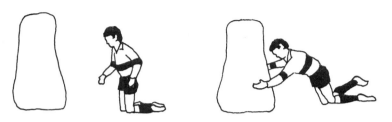

Developing tackling power (1)

Progression
1 Change the start position from kneeling to:

(a) resting on one knee
(b) squatting
(c) crouching and, finally,
(d) standing.

2 Gradually increase the distance of the players from the tackle bag, requiring a powerful drive from the legs to launch the body towards the tackle bag.
3 Players take turns to stand behind the tackle bag and hold it in position, to increase the amount of resistance confronted by the tackler.
4 Remove the bags and insist that players work in pairs, taking turns to tackle each other. Start the practice with both players on their knees; gradually alter the starting position of the player being tackled to a more realistic one, increasing the difficulty of the tackle to include standing, walking and then jogging.

Developing tackling power (2)

Organisation
Players are divided into small groups of three or four; they work in a continuous practice, with one team lined up adjacent to another in a 20 × 20 metre/yard grid area. Players in one team have possession of a ball each, the other team assuming the role of tacklers. The first player in the attacking team walks forwards and the defender tackles the ball carrier from the side. Once the tackle has been completed the players move to the back of the other team and change their roles, enabling each paticipant to experience the success of making a tackle and the effects of being tackled.

Developing tackling power (2)

Coaching points

The attacking player must walk at a brisk but constant pace in a straight line. The defender must quickly assess the speed of the ball carrier and move forwards, either walking or jogging, to make the tackle from the side. He should make contact with the shoulder, driving into a point slightly above the knees of the ball carrier, placing the head behind his thigh and wrapping the arms around his legs. He attempts to grasp the hands together while pulling the arms back towards the chest. The power of the drive, point of contact and timing of the actions will determine whether or not the attacking player is tackled to the ground.

Progression

1 Gradually increase the running speed.
2 Encourage the attacking player to use his repertoire of elusive running skills, making sure that the players remain within the boundaries of the grid area.

Developing tackling power (3)

Organisation
One player stands inside a 10 × 10 metre/yard grid area with four others, who each stand in one corner of the grid. The central player must complete as many tackles as possible in a given period of time before changing places with a corner player.

Coaching points
This is an intensive pressure practice in which the centre player moves as quickly as possible from one corner to another to complete effective and successful tackles. Players will need constant encouragement to ensure that they work at their optimum levels of performance. Inform the players before the start about the length of time of the concentrated period of tackling, which should initially be one minute. Instruct the players to move around the grid in a particular direction to make the tackles, creating the same conditions for everyone. Regularly change the direction of the movement to prevent the players from constantly being tackled on the same side.

Progression
1 Include diagonal runs across the grid so that players will have to perform tackles from the front as well as from the side.
2 Give each of the attacking players a number, calling out the order in which the tackles must be made.
3 Encourage the attacking players to move along the lines of the grid, constantly changing their position.
4 Extend the duration of the concentrated period of tackling.
5 The attacking players move across the grid and can only be tackled when they initially walk, and then later jog, across the central area.
6 Players must complete a certain number of tackles before changing roles.
7 Record the time taken for a player to complete a designated number of tackles; the other participants must then try to beat the previous time.

Developing tackling power (4)

Organisation
Players work in pairs in a 10 × 10 metre/yard grid area with one ball. They stand on the end lines of the grid facing one another. The attacking player has five attempts to reach the opposite line and score a try without being tackled by the defender.

Coaching points
The defending player must react quickly to the movements of the attacking player, attempting to limit the options available by reducing the distance

between the two players. The defender must maintain his balance and control throughout, approaching the ball carrier from an angle, attempting to seize the initiative and make the attacking player run to one particular side of him. Award a point for each try scored and keep a note of the results, punishing the loser with a set number of a particular exercise.

Progression

1 Increase the competition by allowing the tackling player to attempt to dislodge the ball from the hands of the attacking player. If he is successful and able to secure possession, the roles change immediately, discounting any attempts that were remaining.

2 Create 2 v. 2 and 3 v. 2 situations in a grid of the same size, staggering the starting positions of both groups of players. Create further decision-making problems for the tackler including:

(a) the need to isolate the ball carrier from his support
(b) attempting to tackle the player in possession and prevent a pass to a support player from being completed
(c) on failing to prevent the transfer of the ball in tackling one player to the ground, getting up as quickly as possible and attempting to tackle the support player.

3 Increase the size of the grid area to 20×20 metres and the numbers of participants involved, creating 3 v. 3 and 4 v. 4 situations.

Developing tackling power (5)

Organisation

Players work in pairs with one ball in a 10×10 metre/yard grid area. The players run one behind the other, the ball carrier in front and the defender following. The tackling player must complete five tackles before the roles are reversed.

Coaching points

Do not allow players to delay tackles; this should be a concentrated practice, with tackles being performed quickly and the roles being changed regularly. The tackling player must drive powerfully with the legs to increase the power of contact. He should reach his arms around to the front of the ball carrier and pull his legs together, sliding his arms down the legs towards the ankles while retaining a tight grip. The tackling player's head and body should be positioned close to the side of the ball carrier's legs.

Progression: overhaul tackle

This is a technique in which the tackler makes contact from behind, with his shoulder against the upper body of the ball carrier. He should wrap his arms around the player and try to dislodge the ball from his possession by pushing down on it with one hand. The attacking player should be knocked off balance by the combination of the shoulder contact and the arms twisting around his body and pulling him towards the ground.

Development of the unit skills of forwards

This section deals with the unit skills of the forwards and includes practices to develop their ball-winning abilities. Because three-quarters will sometimes be caught in the transitional phases of play of rucks and mauls, they must also be competent in helping to make the ball available to support players to retain possession. Therefore all players need to practise the techniques that help to secure possession for their team in these situations.

However, in the set plays of scrummages and line-outs, the only contribution made by the three-quarters is the service. For example, the scrum-half feeds the ball into the scrummage or, very rarely, some teams use a winger or a scrum-half to throw the ball into the line-out. Therefore during the organisation of these practices the coach can utilise the three-quarters as opposition, which will help to create realistic practice situations for the forwards and develop the abilities of the three-quarters to deal with these different contact aspects of playing.

It is necessary to consider the results of match analysis when preparing the training of forwards because the following information is not only revealing but very pertinent. During a game played over 80 minutes:

1 the ball is only in play for a maximum of 30 minutes
2 there are approximately 40 scrums and 70 line-outs, each lasting between five and 20 seconds
3 the forwards divide their time equally between:

(a) scrummages, line-outs, rucks and mauls
(b) running between 11 and 13 km (six and eight miles), moving from one phase of play to the next, in support of the ball carrier and covering in defence

4 on average the rest periods never exceed forty seconds.

In all of the forward unit skills the key features are:

1 dedicated and concentrated approach
2 collective, co-ordinated effort
3 application to the task of securing possession of the ball
4 willingness to work hard for the benefit of others
5 good body positioning – an understanding and application of the mechanics of movement – being able to drive forwards together and prevent the opponents from achieving the same objective

6 close support
7 good control
8 ability to present and transfer the ball to the scrum-half.

Scrummaging

Participation in the scrummage is physically demanding, with players under considerable pressure to win possession of the ball. The laws of the game clearly define the limitations of the scrummage. It is probably the most influential feature of the game because the outcome of the scrums affects the morale and confidence of the players and determines the tactical approach of teams. Successful and effective scrummaging provides a team with a sound platform and launching point for the execution of many attacking and defensive ploys.

Every forward has a particular role to perform during a scrummage. It is important that the coach helps every player to develop his strength and learn the correct techniques necessary to produce a cohesive unit that is capable of winning controlled possession of the ball.

Key features of scrummaging

1 The feet are correctly positioned if they are both pointing forwards, placed at a comfortable distance apart and firmly on the ground to provide a solid base, supporting the body weight and able to deal with the pressure and extra load caused by the drive of the other players, both team-mates and opponents.
2 Crouch down to lower the centre of gravity and increase stability.
3 Bend the knees to help to produce the power for the forward drive of the legs.
4 Keep the back straight with the head looking forwards.
5 Attempt to keep the hips lower than the shoulders.
6 Binding should be compact, strong and tight. Players can generate tremendous pressure on their opponents by simply pulling together with the hands and arms.
7 Control the ball along the ground and direct it into one of the channels to the scrum-half.

Scrummaging (1)

Organisation
Players work in pairs and scrummage against one another in the centre of a 10 × 10 metre/yard grid area. At a pre-arranged signal by the coach, the players must run to the end of the grid and return to the centre to resume scrummaging against their partner.

The French front row binds together before scrummaging

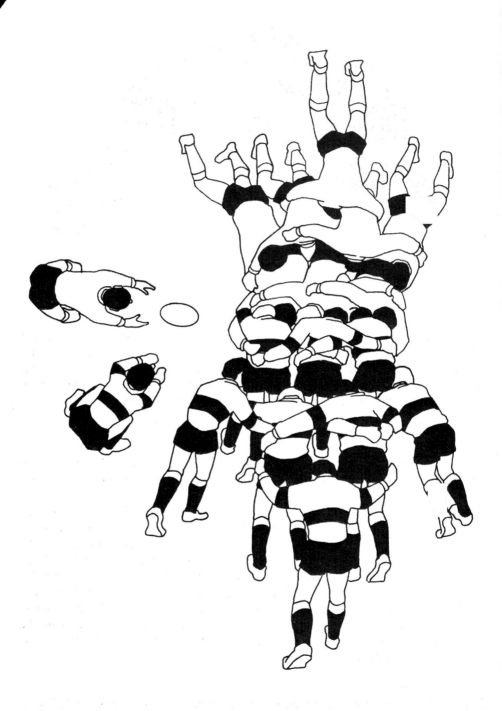

The key features of scrummaging

Scrummaging (1)

Coaching points

There is no need for the players to work with a ball at this stage as they must first concentrate on the mechanics of scrummaging. Take care to avoid any mismatches; whenever possible, players should be paired according to size, strength and weight. It is important to teach the players good habits and technique from the beginning, with the players concentrating on:

1 continuing to look forwards
2 keeping their back straight
3 keeping their legs bent to drive forwards from a solid base of the feet, which should be positioned at least shoulder width apart to maintain good balance.

The players should run to the end line which they are facing, so encourage players to drive their opponent backwards if possible, to reward their efforts by reducing the distance that they have to run to reach the line. On returning to the centre of the grid the players resume the scrummaging contest as quickly as possible. This is a pressure practice but the competitive element should not be responsible for poor technique. Good mechanics and technical application are the key features of successful scrummaging and players must be constantly reminded about their importance. Inform players about the importance of the arms during scrummaging, attempting to lift an opponent off-balance in these direct physical challenges.

Progression

Increase the number of players participating in each grid to create 2 v. 1, 2 v. 2, 3 v. 2 and 3 v. 3 situations.

Scrummaging (2)

Organisation
Players work in small groups of three with one ball in a 10 × 10 metre/yard grid area. Two players scrummage against one another and the third acts as a scrum-half and feeds the ball between the two competing players.

Scrummaging (2)

Coaching points
The players must continue to push against one another but they rest their hands on their knees. When the ball is placed between the players by the acting scrum-half, they attempt to win possession of the ball by pushing it between their legs with their hands. This task requires the players to drive against one another, attempting to push their opponent backwards, move forwards over the ball and maintain good balance. Set a target for the players, keeping a record of the score and changing their roles regularly.

Progression
1 Increase the number of players to create 2 v. 2 and 3 v. 3 situations. It is important that each player binds firmly with the arms and hands with the person on each side before scrummaging against the opponents. When the numbers of players are increased to six, only the central players compete for possession of the ball, using only one foot to guide the ball between the supporting players' legs.
2 Further increase the number of players participating in the scrummage to create 5 v. 5, 6 v. 6, 7 v. 7 and 8 v. 8 situations. By slowly and carefully developing the number of players, the coach can discuss the different positions in the scrummage and the organisation of the players into front row, second row and back row.

Scrummaging (3)

Organisation

A pack of eight forwards works against a scrummaging machine with the scrum-half to practise the execution of sound mechanical technique and the timing of putting in the ball with the striking of the hooker to secure possession.

Scrummaging (3)

Coaching points

This is a specific and concentrated practice to correct any faults in the scrummaging and improve the forwards' ball-winning capabilities. The most common faults are:

1 poor feet positioning, limiting the forward drive and preventing good, controlled channelling of the ball to the back of the scrum

2 inadequate binding
3 poor use of the arms and hands to consolidate the players' strength and contribute to the forward drive when the ball is fed into the scrum
4 players lowering their head, resulting in an arching of the back, which in turn prevents the correct transference of the forward drive
5 poor communication between the hooker and the scrum-half, leading to errors as a result of mistiming the put in and the strike for the ball
6 lack of forward drive from the players when the ball is placed into the scrum.

Constantly encourage players to pull together with the hands and arms to initiate forward momentum, supporting the efforts of the legs when the ball is placed into the scrum. It is important that the wing forwards make extra contributions to the scrummages by:

1 supporting the work of the prop forwards by pushing from the side and behind the prop
2 keeping the feet out wide from the scrum, binding at an angle to protect the scrum-half by delaying the challenges of his opposite number.

Line-outs

This feature of rugby football is a unique method of re-starting the game when the ball has been played into touch. The players stand in two straight lines alongside one another and compete for the possession of the ball. The team not responsible for the ball going into touch has the advantage of the throw in and is able to dictate the length of the line-out, providing the laws of the game are complied with. Unfortunately teams do not exploit the maximum advantage from these opportunities at the line-out, seemingly treating this feature of play as a unit skill that they are not prepared to experiment with or develop in training, to make sure that they secure possession on each occasion that they control the service.

During a scrummage the team feeding the ball into the tunnel between the two teams has a distinct advantage and players work hard in training to make sure that they exploit this situation. Winning the ball against the head is considered a great victory in the direct competitive challenge of the scrummage. However, the line-outs are not held in the same reverence as the scrums and are not given the respect and attention that they deserve, particularly as there are almost twice as many line-outs as there are scrums during a game. Teams must practise the basic drills of throwing the ball as accurately as possible to the recognised jumpers in the line-out, with the other players assuming the role of blockers to prevent opponents from interfering with their possession of the ball. However, executing these basic principles with good timing, communication of signals and teamwork does not guarantee the winning of the ball in the line-out.

The laws of the game also determine that the three-quarters are further apart

England's Wade Dooley out-jumps his French opposite number at the line-out and prepares to flick the ball to his scrum-half, Nigel Melville (number 9)

at the line-outs than during any other phase of play, and they can execute numerous tactical ploys to take advantage of this extra space. Therefore training to improve the winning of good-quality possession from the line-outs could dramatically influence the value of this unit skill to the performance and achievements of a team.

Key features of the line-out

1 Good communication between the player taking the throw in, the other forwards and the scrum-half is crucial.
2 The accuracy and timing of the throw in are vital.
3 Players who do not jump to compete for possession should perform a support role and bind together to prevent the opposition from reaching the ball or breaking through the gaps in the line-out to disrupt the efforts of the scrum-half.
4 The distance of the throw should be varied.
5 Distribution of the ball to the scrum-half must be controlled.

Line-outs (1)

Organisation
Players work in pairs with one ball in a 10 × 10 metre/yard grid area, standing about six metres/yards apart. One player throws the ball accurately towards his partner, who must jump to catch the ball with two hands.

Coaching points
The service of the ball is vitally important and the throwing player must concentrate on accuracy. The receiving player must jump to catch the ball at the

Line-outs (1)

highest possible point and secure possession with a two-handed catch. The feet positions of both players will determine the success of their performance. Both players must point their leading foot towards each other, with the line-out jumper turning his body side on to the thrower. The ball should be held in clear view of the receiver throughout the preparations for the throw, to allow the player in the line-out an opportunity to time his jump for the ball when it is thrown. The receiving player needs to keep his arms relaxed and to the side of his body, to work in conjunction with the legs and drive upwards to catch the ball. When he has caught the ball with two hands, the jumper must turn towards his goal line to help to retain possession by keeping his body between the ball and an imaginary opponent. Alternate the roles after five attempts each, to allow each player to experience the demands of each task.

Progression

1 Introduce a third player to assume the role of the scrum-half, creating a sequence of fluent movement of the ball: the accurate throw in, a good leap to catch the ball and distribution to the scrum-half, who quickly passes to the player throwing in to the line-out.
2 Introduce competition by creating a 1 v. 1 situation in the line-out, with players competing for the ball.
3 Develop the practice into 2 v. 2 and 3 v. 3 situations, with the thrower varying the length of service and the players in the line-out blocking their opponents' attempts to interfere with their possession of the ball.

Line-outs (2)

Organisation

Players work in teams of five or six players, with one ball in a 10 × 10 metre/yard grid area. The players compete with one another in the line-out consisting of three/four forwards standing at least five metres/yards away from the thrower and a scrum-half waiting to distribute the secured possession. Each team has a specific number of throws in to the line-out before their opponents are given the advantage of the service.

Coaching points

The advantage of the service should be exploited to improve the communication and timing of the important players involved, that is, the thrower and the specialist jumpers. The other players should bind closely and support the efforts of the lock forwards to secure the ball, blocking their opponents' attempts to spoil the quality of the possession. Ensure that the players are aware of the laws concerning the line-out and start the practice with the correct distance between the opposing units and each player. All of the players in the line-out should be prepared to react to the throw in, catch the ball if they have the opportunity, and win it for their team. The thrower should vary the distance of the throw, in an attempt to involve all of the players in direct competition for possession. The communications and signals to determine the target area of the throw should be worked out in accordance with the abilities of the thrower and the players in the line-out.

Line-outs (2)

When the players bind to resist their opponents' efforts to reach the ball, they must wrap their arms around either the front or back of the player standing next to them, pulling their bodies close together to create a solid block. The support players must avoid any contact with the ball and improve, not disrupt, the quality of the possession. After catching the ball the player must turn in the air to land facing his scrum-half and crouch quickly to protect it, keeping his body between the ball and the opponents. The support players must bind together and drive forwards into their opponents, attempting to drive them backwards to prevent any efforts to reach the ball. Change over the throw in of the ball after an agreed number of attempts and initially condition the efforts of the opponents to allow the team with the advantage of the service to rehearse their ball-winning capabilities.

Line-outs (3)

Organisation
Carefully position each player in the line-out and work with a scrum-half and the thrower to practise the techniques of the line-out as a unit.

Coaching points
It is important that the players are comfortable with their starting positions in the line-out and are confident that they are in the best place to perform the

specific functions of their playing position. The players with the specific responsibility of securing possession in the line-outs are the lock forwards, supported by the other players, particularly the taller back-row players, who are positioned at the back of the line. This will provide three target areas for the ball to be thrown into the line-out. If teams do not have sufficient tall players with good leg strength, jumping technique and ball-handling skills to provide

Line-outs (3)

successfully three different players as potential target areas for the throw, include different tactical ploys to vary the line-outs and exploit the specific players' line-out strengths by:

1 regularly moving the standing positions of the recognised line-out specialists
2 reducing the number of players standing in the line-out.

These options will allow the players to practise different throw ins, changing the distance and speed of the service of the ball. Players must move into a supporting position, either as soon as the ball travels over their head, or as soon as it is caught by the line-out specialist. When players are convinced that they are able to reach a ball thrown into the line-out they should either attempt to catch it or deflect it with their hands towards the scrum-half. If the ball is not caught at the line-out, specific players (one from the front and one from the back of the line-out to cover all eventualities) should be detailed to sweep around, secure the possession of the ball and distribute it to the scrum-half when requested. Move the position of the line-outs regularly to improve the reaction time of the players.

The throw in

Organisation
The player with the responsibility of throwing the ball into the line-out must practise the technique regularly and in all weather conditions to develop confidence and success in his performance.

Coaching points
Encourage the player to practise individually to improve the accuracy of the throw in. Players can practise by throwing the ball to hit different targets, for example a post or a wall when the specialist line-out jumpers are not available. Once he is accurate at a distance of six metres/yards, the player should increase his distance from the targets. The weather conditions will greatly affect the grip of the ball and its movement in the air after its release. The two main techniques for throwing the ball into the line-out are:

1 bowling action (favoured by some players in the southern hemisphere)
2 torpedo throw.

Players must practise these and any other techniques that they can perform consistently to a high standard to decide on the most suitable. The main criteria

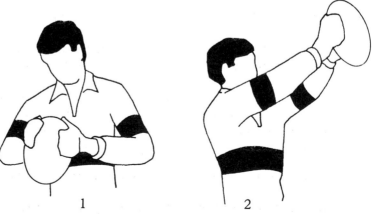

The throw in

3   4   *The throw in*

are accuracy and the ability of the intended receivers to see the ball to time their jump and catch it.

Rucks and mauls

These are the transitional phases of play and are vital to the continuity of the game. Rucks and mauls are formed when there are one or more players from either team competing for the possession of the ball, and they can involve both backs and forwards. It is necessary for the coach and players to discuss the suitability and preferences for one or other of these techniques, to decide whether the players will attempt to ruck or maul the ball once a player has been tackled or is held by an opponent. These two unit skills are fundamentally different in their execution and every player must be aware of and capable of participating in both.

The ruck occurs when the ball is on the ground and it is played back towards the scrum-half using the feet.

The maul occurs when a player manages to stay on his feet when tackled; the ball is held away from the opposition and transferred with a handling movement to a support player.

When a player is tackled by an opponent, the most important factors are that the possession of the ball is retained and there is continuity of forward movement. Players are only confronted with a decision whether to ruck or maul if the ball carrier is strong enough to resist the efforts of the tackler to pull him to the ground.

The decision whether to ruck or maul generally depends on two factors:

1 the ability to keep the ball secure until a support player arrives
2 the individual's upper body and arm strength.

Irish scrum-half Michael Bradley (number 9) receives the ball from a ruck

Key features of the ruck and maul

1 Assume a crouched position to lower the centre of gravity.
2 Continually drive forwards using both legs and arms.
3 Keep the head low to look for the ball and maintain a mechanically sound body position to drive forwards.
4 Good support play is important, with players arriving at the point of breakdown as quickly as possible from behind the ball.
5 Remember that these unit skills are methods of retaining possession – distribute a good ball to the scrum-half at the earliest opportunity.

Rucking

Organisation
Players work in pairs in a 10 × 10 metre/yard grid area with one partner standing in the centre and the other on the end line of the grid. The player in the centre turns away from his partner to keep his body between the ball at his feet and the other player. The player standing on the end line runs towards his partner, makes contact in the small of the back with his shoulder and drives the acting defender beyond the ball, before returning to the start position to repeat the practice.

Coaching points
The driving player must make firm contact by placing his shoulder above the hips of the stationary player and placing his head in a safe place out to the side. He should wrap the arms around the player to help to lift and drive him backwards over the ball. The player protecting the ball must be prepared for the physical collision and relax as much as possible to withstand the impact.

Rucking

Dominique Erbani wins possession of the ball in a maul and is set to pass to Phillipe Dintrans

Change the players' roles after five attempts, to allow both players the opportunity to experience the demands of the task.

Progression

1 Increase the length of the grid to 40 metres/yards to accommodate two further players, standing on each grid line protecting the ball at their feet. This will increase the pressure and requires the players to keep driving and running forwards in pursuit and support of the ball.

2 Change the organisation slightly by insisting that players work in pairs, introducing the need for teamwork, with players joining forces and binding together with their hands and arms before making contact with the stationary defensive players.

Group rucking

Organisation

Players work in large groups of nine members each, sub-divided into three equal teams. Each group takes turns to assume the roles of defenders and attackers. The attacking group starts on the goal line with the defensive groups positioned in front of them, at progressive distances of ten metres/yards away, standing with their backs to the goal line, as if protecting a ball at their feet. The defending players stand with linked arms and are bound loosely together, leaving gaps between themselves. The attacking group of three players runs into each defending group in turn and drives them down the field until the coach signals for them to continue to the next group.

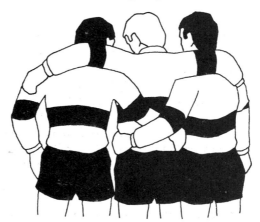

Group rucking: linking and binding

Coaching points

It is vital that the defending players leave gaps for the attacking players to place their heads when making contact and crouching to drive forwards over the imaginary ball. To increase the force of impact to help to continue the forward momentum, the attacking players should slow their running speed on approaching the defending players, link together and drive into the defending players as one group, all making contact at the same time.

Once the attacking players move on to the next group, the defending players must run ahead to resume their stationary position a further ten metres/yards beyond the leading group, continuing for the length of the field. The defending players have to work hard to keep the practice functioning correctly by running quickly between change overs.

It is vital that all attacking players stay on their feet, which means that they must maintain good balance. Players will also need to keep their eyes open to decide where they will place their head. The attacking team members should bind together with the nearest player when joining the ruck and create a scrummage situation, adding depth to the ruck to secure possession. It is important that players drive over the ball and do not attempt to kick it backwards or pick it up when in the ruck. Attempting to kick the ball could have a detrimental effect on the quality of the possession; it will reduce the ability to continue driving forwards and could result in an unfortunate accident to the scrum-half.

Progression
Gradually build up the number of attacking players until the full forward unit is functioning together. The three-quarters can assume the role of the defenders and each group can have a ball for the forwards to drive over and secure possession for their team.

Continuous mauling: taking possession of the ball

Organisation
Players work in groups of three in a 10 × 10 metre/yard grid area with one ball. The players stand at opposite ends of the grid, with one facing the other two players, who have possession of the ball. The ball carrier runs towards the single player and, on reaching the midpoint of the grid, passes the ball to him. On taking possession, the player holds the ball in two hands, level with his chest. The advancing player uses his forearm and shoulder to drive down between the ball and the player's chest to relieve the player of possession. He turns towards the starting point with the ball and continues the practice, running between the players, passing them the ball and then recovering possession.

Coaching points
The concentrated nature of this practice will cause fatigue, but the coach should constantly encourage players and not allow them to lower the standards of performance. Change the roles of the players after ten attempts have been completed. The player holding the ball must keep his head up, in a safe place away from the ball, reducing the risks of any accidents caused by the forearm of the player driving down behind the ball. The advancing player must push the

ball down towards the ground, using his forearm and shoulder as the leading levers to incorporate upper body strength, and crouch down to succeed in dispossessing the player of the ball.

Progression
1 Increase the size of the grid to 40 × 10 metres/yards, with each player standing in a straight line and ten metres/yards apart. The player who is working on securing possession of the ball runs up and down the line passing to each player in turn before taking the ball from them.
2 Introduce a second player to alternate the sequence of players running in support of one another. The player securing possession must make the ball available for his partner to continue the practice.

Mauling (1)

Organisation
Players work in groups of four, with one ball and two tackling bags placed ten metres/yards apart in the centre of a 30 × 10 metre/yard grid area. Two players stand supporting the tackling bags and the other two start on the end line of the grid. The ball carrier runs into the tackling bag, making contact with his shoulder and hip, moving the ball further away from the defender to shield it behind the body. There are several techniques to achieve this objective, but the most straightforward are:

1 moving the ball to the side of his body
2 placing the ball on to the thigh.

These positions will help to secure the ball until the support player arrives to control and totally secure possession further away from the point of impact and thwart any attempts by the defender to gain possession. When the ball is secure,

Mauling (1)

the support player runs to the next tackling bag to continue the practice, with the first player adopting the supporting role.

Coaching points
The ball carrier must stay on his feet and keep driving forwards to continue the forward momentum when in contact with the tackling bag. This can be achieved by standing with the feet wide apart, bending the legs and crouching to create a solid base. It is advisable to introduce only one of the techniques of shielding the ball from the grasp of the tackling player, so that every player is consistent in his technical execution and players will know where to expect the ball to be positioned. Alternate the players' roles so that they move in sequence to the next position, rather than have the same pairs working together all of the time.

Progression
Remove the tackling bags and continue the practice in the same manner, with the defender attempting to stop the ball carrier from advancing forwards.

Mauling (2)

Organisation
Players work in groups of six and form two equal teams. One group assumes the attacking role and advances as a unit with a ball towards the defenders. They stand in different positions, at least ten metres/yards apart in a 40 × 10 metre/yard grid area. Each defensive player must attempt to halt the progress of the attacking unit and prevent them from continuing their forward movement.

Mauling (2)

Coaching points
The ball carrier should run directly into the defender and work hard to maintain good balance and stay on his feet. The ball should be moved away from the defender and made available for the supporting players to secure possession. All of the attacking players should drive into the maul in a low, crouched position, with a straight back and looking forwards. This mechanically sound

body position will enable the attacking players to maintain the forward momentum and consequently limit the efforts of the defender to reach the ball and attempt to secure or disrupt possession.

Progression

1 Gradually increase the numbers of the attacking players until all eight forwards are participating and functioning as a successful unit.

2 Introduce pressure by insisting that each player completes a designated number of exercises before being allowed to participate. This will stagger the arrival of the support players and add realism, resulting in all of the players working harder to achieve the end result, which is continued possession because of good mauling techniques.

3 Gradually increase the number of defensive players to improve their chances of securing possession.

4 Alter the organisation so that the teams are equal in numbers and take it in turns to have possession of the ball and run at their opponents.

Unit skills and team practices

It is vital that coaches prepare their teams for each eventuality that could develop during the playing of rugby football and organise controlled practice situations for each unit to rehearse specific features of play. Both forwards and three-quarters should have an opportunity to familiarise themselves with the particular features of play that they will encounter during their participation in a game. Independent unit practices are invaluable to improve the players' familiarity with colleagues and help them to co-ordinate their efforts to succeed in the execution of each particular task. Concentrated practices to improve the ball-winning capabilities and performances to secure and utilise possession are valuable and very neccessary for every team. During these isolated unit practices each player should be allowed the opportunity to contribute to the application and possible developments of technique that will improve the efficiency of the unit and possibly expand the tactical ploys incorporated in the team plan.

The half-backs

Developing communication

Organisation
The half-backs need to work together as often as possible with a ball to practise and improve the distribution and passing from a selection of different sources of possession, including set pieces and re-starts.

Coaching points
The speed and accuracy of the transfer of the ball from the forwards to the three-quarters is the responsibility of the half-backs. The success of the link between these players depends on the quality of the communication to develop a good rapport and understanding between them. It is important to help these players improve their confidence and respect for each other through continual encouragement and positive criticism. Quick transfer and accurate delivery of the ball from the scrum-half determines the quality of possession for the three-quarters and is crucial to the tactical effectiveness and performance of every team.

Insist that the players complete a designated number of successful passes

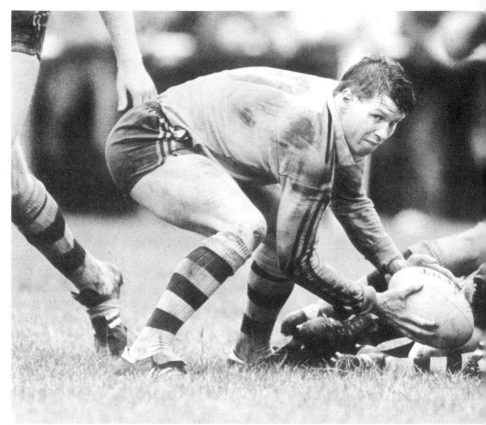

Nick Farr-Jones of Australia prepares to pass the ball to his three-quarters

from each side and from a range of different playing situations and positions. Because the scrum-half determines when the forwards release the ball after securing possession, he should control the tempo of the practice. This can be communicated to the fly-half by counting down from three, with the scrum-half gathering possession of the ball on one. The fly-half should not move until the scrum-half has the ball in his hands. Once the players have completed the set number of passes they should be allowed the opportunity to function independently as a unit and should concentrate their practice together on evolving a discreet code of signals to convey instructions to one another and improve communication.

Progression
1 Encourage the fly-half to increase gradually the distance between the two players to extend the length of pass from the scrum-half.
2 Include a third player into the practice to vary the service and quality of possession given to the scrum-half.

3 Introduce a defender to pressurise the players:
(a) attempting to disrupt the efforts of the scrum-half gathering possession and passing the ball to the fly-half
(b) attempting to distract the fly-half from catching the ball.

Unit skills of the three-quarters

The three-quarters must be constructive in their use of the ball, to penetrate the defence of their opponents, to create better attacking positions and potential scoring opportunities. Unfortunately some players make their role increasingly difficult by creeping forwards in their anxiety to receive the ball. By moving towards the ball, the three-quarters are reducing the amount of space and time that they have available to attack their opponents or execute a tactical passing or kicking movement. It is the responsibility of every player to stop himself from moving forwards, anticipating possession of the ball. The coach can prevent all of the three-quarters from shuffling forwards by restricting any forward movement until the scrum-half has the ball in his hands. Exerting this control will ensure that the three-quarters are patient, hold themselves in check and attack from deep positions.

Good alignment

Organisation
This is a practice to encourage the players to resist the temptation of moving forwards before the ball is under the control of the scrum-half. The three-quarters stand close together in their attacking formation. Either the blind-side winger or a back-row forward provides the service of the ball to the scrum-half

Good alignment

and then runs across the field, attempting to reach the open-side winger before the ball does.

Coaching points

It is important to control the quality of the service from the acting forward and delay his release from the scrum, line-out, ruck or maul, until the ball has been passed by the scrum-half. Also insist that all of the players, particularly the fly-half, remain motionless until the scrum-half has the ball in his hands. Accurate and quick passing along the line of three-quarters will ensure that the ball reaches the winger before the covering defender does. This will instil confidence into the players and will encourage them to remain in deep attacking positions to give them more space and time to function when possession of the ball is secured.

Straight running

Organisation

Four players acting as scrum-halves stand in a straight line approximately 12 metres/yards apart in the centre of the pitch with a ball at their feet. The

Straight running

remainder of the three-quarters are divided equally to stand in two attacking formations on either side of the first scrum-half. All of the three-quarters run straight and pass the ball along the line to the outside player. The fly-half acts as the link player between the scrum-halves and the rest of the three-quarters, zigzagging to join each different line in turn.

Coaching points

This practice revolves around the link between the half-backs and the straight running of the three-quarters to keep the movement flowing. Once the fly-half receives and distributes the ball on one side, he must run between the scrum-halves to link with the other set of three-quarters, receive the second ball and continue the movement. The player running immediately to the outside of the zigzagging fly-half must run straight to prevent the line from running sideways towards the touchline and subsequently out of space. At the start the players must stand with their outside foot pointing in the direction of their intended run; this will enable the players to straighten their running. Once the player on the outside has received the ball he must return it to the scrum-half, allowing the players to continue the practice by turning and running back to the start point.

A two-handed grip gives England's Will Carling plenty of scope to release the ball to the excellent support he has on either side

Passing practice – support running and various tactical ploys

Organisation

The half-backs and all of the three-quarters work together, starting the movement at the half-way line and finishing with a try being scored over the goal line. The object of the practice is to improve the movement of the ball along the line to the outside player and to rehearse different attacking, running and passing ploys to create possible scoring opportunities.

Coaching points

It is important to move the starting position around to different parts of the field, to represent the different phases of forward play that result in possession of the ball, that is, line-outs, scrums, rucks and mauls. This will affect the deployment and alignment of the three-quarters, who must react quickly and move into sensible attacking positions to exploit any possible advantage of each situation. The half-backs must take the responsibility to decide early on the tactical use of the ball and communicate their intended actions to the others. It is necessary to vary the service of the ball to the scrum-half to add realism to the practice, causing a delay of the link pass between the half-backs, which should help players to adapt their timing of a run to execute particular passing movements. Variation of position and service is necessary to make players think and react quickly. Insist that all of the players run in support of the ball once they have transferred it to the next player and encourage close interpassing between the support players before stopping the forward movement to represent a tackle. At the stoppages players must quickly react and return into position to continue the practice, covering for players who are tackled in possession.

The continuity of the practice will teach the players key factors, such as:

1 adaptability
2 the need for good communication and understanding of pre-arranged signals
3 the importance of quick assessment of each different situation
4 decisiveness – good decision making based on the circumstances of each position, involving the availability, positioning and alignment of players
5 the value of good support play.

Experiment with different passing moves to improve the timing and the repertoire of plays that can be executed at particular positions and moments in a game. Scoring opportunities can be created by:

1 switch and dummy switch passes
2 missing players in the line and passing the ball across them to a player who is positioned further away

3 the inclusion in the line of the full-back or one of the wingers, arriving unexpectedly to continue the passing movement of the ball
4 players looping around and supporting the ball carrier.

Attacking and defending skills

Organisation
Units of three-quarters play against one another in half of the pitch, taking turns to control possession of the ball, to practise the effectiveness of their passing moves and defensive tactics.

Coaching points
Each team has possession of the ball for a designated number of attempts and tries to successfully break through the defences of their opponents. At the introduction of this practice condition to touch tackling, that is, a player is tackled when he is touched with two hands by an opponent who is in possession of the ball. Reward each team that scores a try during this competitive practice by either:

1 allowing a further attempt for each try, or
2 punishing the losers by making them complete a number of exercises.

Keep moving the start point of each attempt and vary the source supplying the ball to the three-quarters, that is, alternate between scrum, line-out, ruck and maul. Keep the players informed about the constantly changing source of possession and allow a brief pause before the ball is released to the scrum-half to create realism and allow the three-quarters to signal to one another concerning the intended passing movements and defensive ploys. Make sure that the defending team conform to the laws, compensating for the lack of forwards involved in the practice, that is:

1 they remain at least five metres (yards) away from the scrum-half at scrums, rucks and mauls, as if positioned behind the back foot of an imaginary last player.
2 they are positioned ten metres (yards) away from the line-outs.

Progression
1 Vary the supply of the ball further by giving the ball to the defending team to kick over the heads of the other three-quarter unit of players. This will provide both units with the opportunity to attack, defend and counter attack against the ball kicked into space. The full-back of the unit receiving the kick will rely on his wingers for immediate support when possible to help to initiate a counter attack, with the rest of the players having to turn and run back and move into good support positions to continue the movement.

2 Remove the contact restriction and insist that players tackle one another correctly.

Link between scrum-half and hooker

Organisation

These two players should be given time to work together with a ball, with the hooker scrummaging against one of the goal posts or in the scrummaging machine. Concentrated practice will help these players to decide on the signals that they will use to determine the timing and speed of the ball into the scrummage.

The link between scrum-half and hooker

Coaching points

The hooker determines the factors concerning the feed of the ball into the scrummage. The hooking position involves direct physical contact with the opposition front row, and this competition can delay the player from moving into the most comfortable position to ensure that he reaches the ball first and guides it backwards. Therefore the scrum-half must delay the feed of the ball until the hooker signals. Each hooker should inform the scrum-half of particular preferences concerning:

1 the time that the ball should be held in position where both hookers can see the ball
2 the speed of the service.

The scrum-half must apply these individual preferences at each put in, contributing to his team winning the ball when they have the advantage of the service. The players should agree on different signals to help to communicate with one another when their opponents are about to put the ball into the scrum to try to win the strike of the ball.

Progression
Introduce the prop forwards to support the hooker and gradually increase the number of players participating in the scrummage to improve the players' familiarity with one another.

The forwards as a unit

Opposed pressure practice

Organisation
A pack of eight forwards works with a scrum-half and one ball in a grid that is half the size of the playing area, completing a series of unit drills against other players and possibly a scrummaging machine.

Coaching points
This is an exhausting practice that requires concentrated effort from all the players and considerable encouragement from the coach. It is important that each unit skill is performed efficiently and successfully to secure the possession of the ball, which should be distributed accurately and effectively to the scrum-half. The players should move as quickly as possible from one situation to the next and position themselves correctly for the requirements of the particular unit skill, whether line-out, scrummage, ruck or maul. The distance between each phase of possession need only be 20 metres/yards to allow the players to regroup and concentrate on the execution of the unit skill.

The opposition players need to be conditioned and controlled in their attempts to compete for possession and resist the efforts of the pack of forwards. Either continue the practice for a designated period of time, or until a targeted number of ball-winning contests is completed. Do not allow the players to delay their involvement in any of the unit skills; match analysis has shown that the maximum rest period between activity periods is only 40 seconds and this knowledge should be the key feature of this practice.

Progression
Extend the period of time or the number of unit skills that must be completed before the players are allowed to rest.

Re-starts – kick-offs and drop-outs

Organisation
The forwards work in conjunction with the player(s) who are responsible for kicking the ball to re-start the game. It is important to practise both the place kick and drop-kick re-starts at the half-way line, as well as the drop-outs from

the 22-metre (25-yard) line, because the laws require different criteria for each particular re-start.

Coaching points

Make sure that all of the players are aware of their role during these re-starts. The most important factor concerning these kicks is that they are executed correctly and concur with the laws of the game. A re-start kick should never go directly into touch because the other team will be given the option of receiving the kick again, or of having the distinct advantage of the feed into the scrummage in the centre of the respective re-start line. The player(s) will need to regularly practise the techniques of the re-start kicks to ensure that the opportunity to regain and secure possession of the ball is exploited. The tallest players, usually the lock forwards, sometimes supported by the Number 8, should be the target and spearhead of the attack to run and jump to catch the ball from the re-starts. The front row players should support these target forwards, to block the efforts of the other team and help to secure possession. The back row players will constitute the third wave of support, arriving at the catching point as quickly as possible, to help to continue the forward drive and momentum.

It is also necessary to rehearse the defensive ploys that will be employed when receiving the kick. Again, every player will need to be aware of his position to receive the re-start kicks, spread around the expected target area to cover as much of the ground as possible to prevent the kicking team from gaining any advantage. As soon as the kick is taken and the players have assessed the landing area of the ball, they should move as quickly as possible to support the receiving player. Before re-starting the kicker needs to assess the weather conditions, because these will affect the direction and flight of the ball and the power needed to produce a successful kick. Players must be behind the ball when it is kicked and can use the space to time their run, so that they are moving from behind the ball, to generate the speed needed to improve the height that they are able to jump off the ground to reach the ball.

Progression

Experiment with different types of re-start kicks, for example:

1 kicking deep towards the opponents' goal line
2 switching the direction of the kick
3 keeping the ball low along the ground.

Touch rugby

Organisation

The size of the playing area can be altered depending on the number of players involved and the amount of pressure that the coach wants to include.

Coaching points

Players enjoy touch rugby because it provides an opportunity to refine handling and running skills without the demands of physical contact or rigorous tackling. A player is considered tackled when he is touched with two hands by a defender when in possession of the ball. By restricting the number of tackles before a team must hand over possession to the other team, both sides are allowed the possibility of practising the following skills:

1 quick transference of the ball
2 running:
(a) in possession of the ball
(b) in support of the ball carrier, and
(c) to cover other players and defend.

This game helps players to improve the speed at which they are able to assess situations and develops their decision making and judgement. The smaller the size of the teams, the greater the levels of concentrated involvement, which will help to improve the abilities and fitness of those involved. Players are able to develop both attacking and defending skills, while hopefully appreciating the necessity for good passing and support play. The coach should prepare the players in advance about an agreed signal or command that will stop a game at any moment, freezing the action and positions of the players as quickly as possible. Enforcing this condition will allow the coach to highlight particular attacking opportunities or defensive plays. It is important that the games are played between players of similar standards and that mismatches of abilities are avoided. This will ensure that all players will need to work hard.

Unopposed/opposed rugby

Organisation

Both units of players, the three-quarters and the forwards, join forces to work together as a team and use the whole pitch to play a continuous game of rugby.

Coaching points

The coach determines which activities are included, that is, method of re-start kick; when players are tackled to form a ruck or maul; when an error occurs for a scrummage to take place and so on, to include as many different situations as possible for the players to experience and rehearse set plays, unit skills and penalty moves. At the beginning, run the practice several times without any opposition, constantly regulating and monitoring the situations, informing players of the changing situations, positions and attacking possibilities.

Progression

1 Gradually introduce opposition into key playing positions to add realism, but carefully control the degree of contact between the players.
2 Occasionally reverse the players' roles.
3 Remove the contact condition to include tackling when both teams have an equal number of players.

Index